Inspired & Outspoken

Inspired & Outspoken

THE COLLECTED SPEECHES OF ANN WIDDECOMBE

EDITED BY
JOHN SIMMONS

WITH A BIOGRAPHICAL PREFACE
BY NICK KOCHAN

First published in Great Britain 1999
by Politico's Publishing
8 Artillery Row
London
SW1P 1RZ
United Kingdom
Tel 0171 931 0090
Email politicos@artillery-row.demon.co.uk
Website http//www.politicos.co.uk

A catalogue record of this book is available from the British Library

ISBN 1902301226

Printed and bound in Great Britain by St. Edmundsbury Press
Cover Design by Ad Vantage

Publisher's Note

At the request of Ann Widdecombe, who receives no payment, we are donating a share of the proceeds of this book to ZOCS.

ZOCS (Zambian Open Community Schools) provides schools and education in Zambia for those whose families can not afford the fee to attend Government Schools. On a visit to the country this Easter Ann saw at first hand the conditions experienced in Chiboyla Open Community School, which is situated near Lusaka. It was without any furniture or materials. The children sat on stones and learned by rote. There were no books, pencils or even a blackboard, as the school was occupying a church and so could not store any property.

Ann has promised to help raise funds for a new building, furniture and educational equipment. Individual donations (cheques payable to ZOCS) may be sent c/o Rt Hon Ann Widdecombe MP, House of Commons, London, SW1A 0AA or direct to ZOCS, PO Box 50429, Lusaka, Zambia and marked on the back "Chiboyla School".

Contents

Editor's Note

I am grateful to Ann Widdecombe for allowing us to compile this collection of her speeches and articles. Although the selection and editing process has been undertaken by me alone I could not have achieved this without Ann's willing co-operation and advice. I am also indebted to Nick Kochan for undertaking to write a short biographical essay on Ann. He has produced exactly what was asked of him and I hope his words enable the reader to understand a little better what lies behind the feisty politician whom we have come to admire.

So why have we published this book? For the simple reason that Ann Widdecombe represents a breath of fresh air in modern political life. She speaks her mind with barely a care for the consequences. We need more politicians who are less bothered about the future of their careers and more concerned about the welfare of the nation.

Ann's rise to national prominence has hardly been meteoric. Typically it was an issue of conscience which brought her to national prominence as a woman of principle and conscience. Since the 1997 electoral debacle Ann has become a star of the Conservative front bench. She is seen as the de facto deputy leader of the Conservative Party and has done more than most to galvanise the Party faithful.

Her starring role in fighting the Government over the summer of 1999, when she appeared to take on the entire Government front bench single-handedly won her deserved plaudits. For the first time in two years Home Secretary Jack Straw was put on the back foot. During a sound test prior to a TV interview on the subject of asylum seekers she said memorably: "My name is Ann Widdecombe. This morning I had Straw for breakfast." Quite. I commend her words to you.

JOHN SIMMONS
August 1999

Nick Kochan

Ann Widdecombe's Winning Conscience

The uncrowned deputy leader of the Conservative Party is small, practically dressed to a fault, and tidy. Her hair must be groomed into that familiar style, her dress perfectly prim and her toe nails polished. Ann Widdecombe may make no effort to be fashionable, but she would never want to seen by the public untidy.

The pressures of getting up early to drive herself down to her Maidstone constituency have not affected the Shadow Home Secretary's impressive capacity for vitriol and analysis. Ann Widdecombe's energy levels are as high as they were at the start of the day. She is bustling around her office, demanding coffee, real coffee and now.

Widdecombe is ready to lay into the morals of the present Labour leadership with a gusto rare among politicians. She is also eager to rubbish their policies, while admitting that those of the opposition are in the discussion and research stage and not yet fully fledged. Love her or hate her, Ann Widdecombe is right there, and itching to go.

The toughness which gave rise to the now notorious 'Doris Karloff' tabloid nick-name dates back to her sturdy defence in 1996 of the hospital and prison system over the manacling of pregnant women in maternity wards. Her ferocious row with former Home Secretary, Michael Howard, over his account of the sacking of the Prisons chief Derek Lewis kept her in the public eye. She has not left it since.

Widdecombe deals with the Doris Karloff barb with her phlegmatic brand of humour. 'The most sensible thing you can do when a campaign is running in the press is adopt it. I used to pick up the phone and say Karloff here. It is the exact thing you would say to a child who is being laughed at. Call yourself fatty, and don't look hurt because if you do they enjoy it more. It was really water off a duck's back. I wouldn't have been so sanguine in the first week I entered politics, but you get used to it.'

Ann Widdecombe's life long climb up the greasy pole has been accomplished without the benefit of rich parents, political heritage or powerful mentors. In some senses, she is an heir to Margaret Thatcher, but a generation later, sharing a number of the former Prime Minister's characteristics, namely aggression, straight speaking and ambition. But the parallel should not be pushed too far. Widdecombe's religious and moral attitudes differ markedly from Thatcherite economic individualism. In any event Widdecombe, more than most politicians, makes a point of being her own woman - not part of a clique or a crowd.

Ann Noreen Widdecombe was born in 1947 in Bath, the second child of a civil servant. Her father's work in naval armaments kept the family on the move during Ann's early years. They moved both inside Britain and abroad, and by the time she was eleven years old, she had attended no less than five schools, including the Royal Naval School in Singapore, one of her father's postings. Ann's brother Malcolm was considered old enough to stay on his own at school in Britain during these years, so Ann was on her own with her parents. Such upheaval might have upset less robust girls, but Ann found it exciting. 'Every time we moved, I was off to a new house, a new school and everything was fearfully exciting. I think it helped that we did live in a series of quite interesting houses.'

The moving stopped when Ann was eleven, and her parents put her into Bath Convent as a day girl. The choice of a Catholic school was not immediately obvious as the Widdecombes were

Anglican and her mother was from a Baptist family although she later became a committed Anglican. But Bath Convent had good academic standards and was regarded as 'strict'. It also had a boarding part of the school, and in due course Ann would become a boarder to save her education further disruption when the family moved yet again.

That Ann should be sent to a religious school rather than a secular one was not surprising. Religion ran deep in the Widdecombe family. Her grandfather was a lay reader, her uncle a vicar, and her father a regular attender at Church. Her mother and brother had 'religious enthusiasm' in their bones, but her father went more out of habit. Ann's brother followed the family tradition and became a vicar.

As far as Ann's development was concerned, the important point is that she felt part of a minority and, being Ann, she would not be ground down by it. 'I had to stand up for myself. In the early Sixties, before the Vatican Two debate, conflict was rife between the Anglican and Catholic Churches. There was huge distrust between the churches. If you were Catholic, you could not go into an Anglican church without a special dispensation. As far as the Anglicans were concerned, Rome was something very foreign and subversive and not quite right. Now of course that spirit of hostility has almost completely disappeared. I can remember the beginning of the ecumenical movement, when everybody was talking about this as if it were something very big and new and serious. Now we all take it for granted. There was undeniably a conflict there. It toughened me up.'

Ironically, given her later change, she found the Catholic practices at the time repellent. 'I left school very, very anti-Catholic. I regarded the religion as hopelessly superstitious and full of ritual. And I held quite strongly to that view. I was strongly Protestant and Anglican.' Ann was confirmed when she was 18 in the Anglican Church in Bath Abbey, and determined to commit herself to the Anglican church.

In the meantime, she had started to become immersed in two

other spheres of activity: politics and Latin. Ann's interest in politics started to show itself when she was around fourteen. From the start she followed her family's Conservative leanings. Neither of her parents was active politically, her father for reasons of his career. The origins of her Conservatism are straightforward: 'The whole family's Conservative in fact; the immediate family. I have some fairly rabid Labour cousins. It's very deep in me. I am one of nature's Conservatives; I do believe in as little role as possible for the state, as much role as possible for the individual. I am innately Conservative, not in the sense of always wanting to preserve what is there, but Conservative in the sense of the values of the individual versus the state. Even if my views on various things have changed over the years, I've never had anything other than an interest in Conservatives.'

Her view of politicians at the time was romantic and idealistic. 'I thought that all politicians were like Winston Churchill, and that they all had great places in history.' By the end of her teens she had revised this view and was considerably more realistic, having joined the Young Conservatives and seen some politicians in the flesh. She now insists she has no mentors or political idols, although she has always been impressed by Lord Hailsham.

The makings of the early politician were also evident in her early capacity to excel at debating. She was chairman of the school's debating society and won a first class award at the Mid Somerset festival public speaking competition. She later got the 'McKee' cup for debating while at university.

Ann's other passion while at school was for the arts, not the sciences. Like an earlier distinguished right-wing Conservative Enoch Powell, she studied the Classics, especially Latin where she was quite precocious. She was in the fast stream, and did four A levels, Latin, Ancient History, History and English over three years. She also did some Greek. Sciences were an anathema, and she candidly admits she was 'lousy at maths.'

She was also a 'disaster' at sport, and did not engage in such frivolities as acting, or singing. She did however become a house captain. As she made clear when she appeared on Desert Island Discs in 1999, she is tone deaf. However, at a school which expected some musical effort from its young women, Ann learnt to sight read, using her formidable memory to compensate for what she lacked in natural musical talent.

It was natural that Ann would want to study Latin, not quite so obvious that she would go to one of the country's 'Red Brick' universities. But Oxford was elusive at this point, and she chose to study at Birmingham, which had an excellent Classics department. There she followed a similar path to the one she had taken at school - hard academic work, more debating, and an active interest in Christianity. She joined the University's Christian Union, and was fascinated by the Billy Graham evangelical crusades, then all the rage. Politics was confirmed as her enduring passion, and while at Birmingham, she decided she wanted to embark on a political career.

Her upper second class degree was sufficient to allow her to enter the country's great political seed bed of Oxford, and in 1969 she went up to Lady Margaret Hall to read for another first degree, this time in PPE, politics, philosophy and economics. She followed in the footsteps of many politicians by joining the Oxford Union, and seeking its presidency. She was beaten there by Patric Dickinson, the later Richmond Herald at the College of Arms. All the same she became the Union's secretary and treasurer. Ann encountered many of the leading Conservatives of the day at Oxford, including the leader of the party, Edward Heath. On one occasion, the two were together alone for six or seven minutes before he entered the debating chamber. She says she was able to make little headway in conversation with the notoriously monosyllabic elder statesman. The Conservatives won the 1970 general election, and much to Ann's delight, Edward Heath became Prime Minister. In fact Ann Widdecombe supported Heath's unsuccessful campaign to retain the leadership against Margaret Thatcher in 1975. 'I stood up for Ted Heath because I reckoned that he had been badly let down by the country. He said "Who rules?". He was one of the earliest to ask that central question about the trade unions. The country didn't return him an answer, and I thought he'd been very badly let down. I was actually loyal to him in that leadership battle, needless to say I now think that the best thing that could have happened to the Tory party was if Margaret Thatcher did win. But it is no good pretending that I foresaw that at the time, because I didn't. I didn't foresee that she was going to have such a massive impact.' Ann Widdecombe kept her counsel about the new leader for some time after her election, only really accepting she was a winner with the electorate as the 1979 election hove into view.

In terms of ideology, the right-wing Widdecombe was no ally of Heath. But neither was she a soul mate of Margaret Thatcher. Her moral stands on issues like abortion and the family overlapped little with Margaret Thatcher's economically-oriented individualism.

The central plank of Widdecombe's platform from the earliest stage was abortion. Her passion on the subject had been expressed many times to students at Birmingham and Oxford. She saw abortion as 'killing children', and it was abhorrent. 'Abortion to me is a major issue of protecting the unborn child. It has nothing to do in that sense with sexual morality, my concern is the child. It doesn't matter if that child is the product of a legitimate or illegitimate liaison. My objection to it is that it is killing.' The liberalisation of abortion permitted by the 1967 Act caused her 'total horror' and she was a tireless campaigner, as early as she can remember, on behalf of the Society for the Protection of Unborn Children, to have the Act changed.

The passion for politics, and the determination to have a career as a Member of Parliament, was well and truly unleashed at Oxford but Ann Widdecombe had still to earn money to deal with the basic necessities of life. She spent a short time at Oxfam (when she went down from University), and then two and a half unpleasant years in the marketing department at Unilever. She found marketing special soaps to people who did not need them pointless.

Both she and Unilever were glad when she quit the commercial world as soon as another opening presented itself. While she admires people who 'make money', she says, she is somebody who has to 'earn' it. That opening was at the University of London, The comfortable world of academic administration was not merely more congenial intellectually - she was working on the financial implications of the many hospital and medical school mergers that were already underway - but it also gave her the time to pursue that first love, politics. Politics occupied the evenings, weekends, and holidays, and every available moment in between. 'I used all my spare time for politics. The whole lot. That was one of the attractions for me. When I presented myself at my first seat, I was able to say to them "Yes, I can put in lots of time".'

The grown-up political world first encountered Ann Widdecombe when she served as personal assistant to Michael Ancram when he was running his election campaign in the Scottish Borders during the second general election of 1974. But shortly after that she made her own debut, winning a councillor's seat on the Runnymede District Council in Surrey, where she was living at the time. She was a local councillor there from 1976-78, promoting vigorously the right of council house owners to buy their homes, and she produced a leaflet to that effect.

She made her first attempt at entering parliament in 1979, when she stood in the safe Labour seat of Burnley. She nursed the constituency for 18 months before the election, going there every weekend. The fruit of her effort was a halving of the Labour majority. The energy and devotion that would become her hallmark were starting to impress members of her party who read her Bow Group pamphlets on subjects like aids for the deaf, candidate selection (a topic on which, through bitter experience, she was well qualified to speak!), general health issues and disability.

The path towards a safe seat would prove elusive. Next time around, in 1983, Widdecombe was selected to fight Devonport against a formidable opponent in David Owen. Owen had only recently broken away from Labour to form the Social and Liberal

Democrats and he was riding the crest of a wave. The only compensation for challenging such a big name was the media interest he drew to the constituency, as well as the big name speakers like David Steel who came to support his cause. Some of the coverage rubbed off on the Conservative candidate. 'It was a bit like a by-election. It was good fun. We didn't win, but it was good fun.' Looking back she says she has 'quite a respect for David Owen, so it's probably just as well I didn't win!'

Her record of standing and losing valiantly, put her in line for the next safe seat when it became vacant. That would be the seat of Maidstone in Kent. The experience of victory in 1987 would be sweet. 'I remember being absolutely ecstatic that I'd got there at last. It had been a very long haul, I had been through scores of selections. So I was very glad to be there, because it was a seat that looked as if it could be held. I felt very optimistic about the future and I set out to enjoy myself.'

The period of Widdecombe's entry to Parliament was momentous in more ways than one. Coinciding with the achievement of a long sought-after career goal was a personal change, indeed clarification of purpose, that would renew her inner strength. For a decade off and on, Ann Widdecombe's faith had been waning to the point where she says now she was completely agnostic and had stopped going to Church.

She describes the loss of faith: 'Becoming an agnostic was a gradual of erosion of belief and coming back from agnosticism was a gradual erosion of unbelief'. At either end of that scale, probably, I would have said to you, one day "yes I'm a Christian, yes I'm an Agnostic", not because I was fluctuating all the time but because it was gradual.

'I didn't use the word agnosticism in the 'woolly' sense that it's used now. When people say "I'm agnostic", they mean "I don't know". An agnostic actually takes a position which says, "Man can have no knowledge beyond material phenomena.' It is an actual intellectual position.

'I certainly never became an atheist, because to me, atheism is supremely illogical—you cannot prove a great negative. It is quite difficult to experience the absence of God. When you say, 'I haven't yet managed to discover him' it is not logical to conclude, 'therefore he does not exist'. It is an amazing 'negative' to be able to assert, and I do not see that it is capable of proof. But I do believe you can prove a positive which you can experience yourself.'

What triggered this period of doubt is obviously complex and highly personal. But one element for Ann, was puzzlement leading to disappointment at some of the statements of the leaders of the established Anglican church. She traces the first shock to the moment in 1978 that Hugh Montefiore was appointed Bishop of Birmingham, only weeks after he had mooted the possibility that Christ could have been homosexual. Then her despair was redoubled when the Bishop of Durham was allowed to keep his job 'while questioning every article of creed'. 'I started to think: "I don't like this, I want a church that actually believes in this, or doesn't", there's no point in standing up and saying the creed in Durham if your Bishop is preaching against it. It seemed to me that promotion in the Church of England was dependent on how far you departed from Christian teaching. The quicker and further you departed, the quicker you got promoted.'

The moment she returned to the faith was as elusive as the time she questioned it, 'there was no flash of light' she asserts, but her belief in God was as assured and strong as before. Where there is a puzzle is why she stayed with the Anglican Church, and did not take the leap into the Catholic Church at this point, and not later. 'I came back as an Anglican, I didn't come back as Catholic. That was a phenomenal mistake. You would have thought I could have detached myself sufficiently to have made a judgement. All the time that I was outside the Church I was looking at the Church, in despair at the Anglicans but quite admiring Rome. And I think I came back as an Anglican partly due to mental laziness—because I'd always been an Anglican, therefore it was fairly easy to come back as an Anglican.' Five years later she would rethink that decision.

In fact when she entered Parliament in 1987, and joined the supporters of David Alton's Abortion Bill the Private Member's Bill that won that lottery for parliamentary time in that parliament— she received most help from the Catholics, and less than she had hoped from the Anglican Church, confirming her doubts about the Anglican intentions. Such was her enthusiasm for Alton's measure that some were left with the impression (referred to even today) that abortion was Widdecombe's only interest. 'I think a lot of people saw me as a 'single issue' politician. I had something of that image to throw off.'

But the problem was one of image and not conviction. She has no doubt whatsoever that a substantial part of the public was supporting her's, and Alton's stance. 'I have always thought, (and I cannot prove) that the majority of people share my view. They might not go as far as me; they might not say "no abortion", but I think quite a high majority share my view that abortion's gone too far. I get that impression. It's not a 'party' political issue. It was David Alton's Bill, and David's a Liberal, and other people on that side of the argument, people like Dale Campbell-Savours, now Joe Benton and Kevin McNamara, would have been allies in that fight.'

There are, of course, many other moral causes that Widdecombe supports strongly. Foremost among them are her opposition to the reduction in the legal age for homosexual consent and the easing of conditions for divorce. Later she went public on her opposition to fox hunting. Above all else, she is a stout defender of marriage and the traditional family. While her views on society and individual behaviour are undoubtedly held by people not sharing her religious convictions, her private religious beliefs at some level must underpin the values and morality she espouses. 'You can't have a society with people just doing what they like without any value being placed on self-restraint. Instant gratification very rarely brings happiness. Happiness is something you work towards, and it is a by-product of other things, of a contented marriage, having a good career, having children you love. Happiness is a by-product, it is not something you get in one night's fun.

'The essence of my social views is that marriage is the foundation of society, and that I believe that is what policy should be centred around. I do not believe that the licence of the 60s and 70s has made for a happier nation. We have a very high rate of divorce which is scarcely a measure of happiness. We have a very high rate of teenage pregnancy and teenage sexual ill health, presumably they are not all ecstatically happy. We have a high rate of suicide. We do not have a happy society as a result of unbridled licence, and I never expected us to. The views I hold now were the views I held in the 60s and 70s and I couldn't see it leading anywhere except to disaster.'

The debate over the Alton Bill gave the backbencher a chance to come to the notice of the Government powerbrokers, and it was only a matter of time before she would be marked out for promotion. But she would have to wait for Margaret Thatcher to depart before her wish would be fulfilled.

In fact, Widdecombe supported the Prime Minister's cause when she was challenged in 1990. When she lost the leadership of the party and of the country, Widdecombe was disappointed, but the two formidable women never quite gelled. Indeed later on, when Widdecombe was given a government job, Margaret Thatcher had little to say to her. 'On two separate occasions I stood next to Mrs Thatcher in the lobbies, she never said 'congratulations' and she never said 'thank you for helping my campaign' and it wasn't rudeness, it was that she was just detached from the people immediately around. So I don't think she knew who I was. Unfortunately it was part of the downfall; if she had been more engaged, if she had done what John Major did almost every night of his life, which was to walk through the lobby talking to people, I think she would probably have been there for a lot longer.'

John Major during his inaugural reshuffle put Ann Widdecombe on the first rung of the ministerial ladder. Like everyone else in Parliament, and many in the country, the new Prime Minister was coming to terms with the arrival of a new ferocious debater to Westminster. But Ann Widdecombe tells a touching story about how the famously unassuming John Major and she bumped into each other for the first time.

'One Saturday night, when I was a back bencher, I was sitting in a fish and chip shop in Kennington, I was in my ancient clothes because I'd either been decorating or gardening. I was reading a novel by Douglas Hurd, and I was waiting for my kebab, and suddenly somebody came and sat down opposite me. I looked up and it was John Major, he was Chief Secretary at the Treasury at the time. He started to engage with me in conversation, I thought "I know who this is but I'm not quite sure". I was very new. And then I got it. He knew who I was although it was very early on.'

The chance encounter was marred however, at least as far as Widdecombe was concerned, when Major insisted on telling her the end of the Hurd novel. ' I said, "thanks very much!" The fish and chip shop, with its special line in kebabs, was the venue for many meetings between the two Conservative stalwarts, until John Major became Prime Minister, and he doubtless had his takeaways brought to him.

Ann Widdecombe's first job in government was not quite the one she had expected, or frankly, hoped for. She was appointed Parliamentary Under Secretary of State in the Department of Social Security working to Tony Newton, with particular responsibility for pensions. Her first thoughts, rarely the best, were that it would be 'terribly dry and dull.' This would be proved quite wrong. In fact, the pensions portfolio would turn out to be unexpectedly challenging.

She could not have known that shortly after taking up the job, Robert Maxwell would topple off the side of his boat. Company pensions would go to the top of the news bulletins and compensating the Maxwell victims was at the head of her agenda. Pension mis-selling was also hoving into view during her tenure, showing her the dubious working of an industry which was quite new to her. Then, there were the implications for pensions of the equalisation of retirement ages for men and women. Overarching all these tactical problems was the intractable policy issue of the cost of paying for the state pension. Widdecombe: 'How do you sustain a system which is pay-as-you-go - I mean we take national insurance today and pay it out today as pension, but there's no fund building up - when the elderly population is expanding and the working population is shrinking?' Neither Widdecombe nor any subsequent Labour or Conservative government has sorted out that conundrum.

When Widdecombe heard the news of Maxwell's death she did not give it a second thought. 'But about a week later the pensions thing exploded and we realised it had a very great deal to do with social security.' Widdecombe was at the government helm steering through some very emotional as well as technically complicated areas of company pensions law.

Maxwell presented the ministry with two particular problems: compensating victims of the fraud; and restoring confidence in the pensions industry. Widdecombe realised the extent of the losses suffered by Maxwell pensioners when she was brought face to face with Ivy Taylor, a lady of some years whom she calls (with great affection) 'a battleaxe'. In fact, the *Daily Mirror* arranged for Ivy Taylor to confront the Minister at the Conservative Party Conference. But the stunt failed when Ivy threw her arms round Widdecombe, and told her how pleased she was to see her.

While Widdecombe's sympathies were clearly with the victims of the fraud, the robbed pensioners, there was no question of putting her hand indiscriminately into government coffers to compensate them. 'We had to say "well hang on, there are people who owe the Maxwell company, there are assets there, that's what has got to be liquidated, and then tell us what we're short for."

'There was no question of the government underwriting a

massive theft', she says.

The government also needed to put some support behind an industry that was reeling from public criticism, and experiencing a temporary 'crisis of confidence'. Widdecombe was the reassuring support in a storm, calming the public's fears about other Maxwells lurking in the shadows. Their pension money was quite safe, she told the press. 'Maxwell was the exception. Pensions are as safe as houses, quite honestly they're like banks. Every so often you get a big bank robbery but it doesn't mean you lose confidence in the banking system. This was the first real, big pensions robbery.'

If Maxwell was a big surprise, the government had much more notice of the forthcoming row over the mis-selling of pensions. For over a year, the Treasury and the Department for Social Security had received evidence of isolated cases of people tempted out of their occupation pensions by the offer of private pensions. They had later discovered that they had been disadvantaged by the change and looked to the government for explanation. The government had been encouraging people without pensions to buy private pensions and the whiff of scandal was the last thing the government needed.

The pensions regulators mollified Widdecombe, but only for a short time.'They assured me that everything was all right. I had my suspicions that it was not; Treasury had its suspicions that it was not. And indeed about a year later we had the solid evidence that it was not. We started finding people of the wrong age who should never have come out of occupational pension schemes. Never. We'd advised the pension companies not to get people out of occupational pension schemes, which are about the best value that's going. But to get people who had no access to occupational pension schemes, to bring them in to the private pensions system.'

As the cases multiplied, the government tightened up some of the procedures, but there was only a limited amount that the law could do. 'There was this feeling "yes, we've done that, but we're not quite sure". Her conclusion was that there was only a very limited extent to which the government could get involved - a view largely confirmed even by the new Labour government with its naming and shaming policy. Her typically robust conclusion: 'A few greedy people perverted the whole thing. Not politicians.'

Proposals to equalise the age at which both men and women should be eligible for the state pension were touted while Widdecombe was at pensions. The favoured solution was to leave it up to the individual employee, and allow him or her to choose an age between 60 and 70. But Widdecombe came out against it on cost grounds. 'It was going to cost volumes because effectively everybody would retire at the lower end' and the government settled on 65.

The pensions department thrust Widdecombe into an area where an understanding of human issues as well as complex matters of law and finance was required. She provided it, although she puts down some of her success there to her civil servants, whom she has no hesitation in calling the best she has encountered in government. ' I was dealing with top rate people in Social Security who had no political agenda. Their agenda appeared to be the integrity of the social security system. It was probably the only department I've been in where there was no obvious underlying political agenda. And they were very bright, they were fearsomely bright that bunch.'

The period of the early nineties was not merely one of political challenge, and indeed success, for the Minister. It was also one where her religious thinking, and in particular her dissatisfaction with the Church of England, was beginning to crystallise. In the five years since she had returned to an active belief in God, she had seen the Church of England move yet further away from its roots. The last straw for her, as it was for many, was the vote in November 1992 in favour of the ordination of the women. She decided then that the Anglican Church was not for her, and she announced she was leaving. Six months later she joined the Catholic Church. It was a move where Cardinal Hume was a strong support and influence and she has no doubt it was the right decision. 'I feel much more spiritually content. I feel as if I have been a Catholic always. On my death bed I shall say that was my best decision.'

Cardinal Hume is one of only three people Widdecombe has met whom she feels are 'truly holy'. The other two are the current Pope and Mother Teresa. Her meeting some years later, following her conversion, with the Pope was a powerful if unexpected event. 'I was going to Rome on Home Office business, it was a European issue. I said to officials, "could you see if you could get me a Papal audience". I got a message back saying, "yes, you can have an audience". I was over the moon, but I seriously thought that I would be in a line of twenty and I would shake a hand. I couldn't believe it when I was shown in, and not even a private secretary stayed, nobody stayed. It was just him and me, solo. He spoke very good English. Amazing! Amazing! I came out feeling not entirely on this earth. He is a very, very holy man."

The single quality that binds Widdecombe's religion and her politics is great energy and positive thinking. But she struggled to get enthusiastic about her next posting in the Department of Employment where John Major moved her in 1993. The move was parallel rather than upwards, and a little less exciting than she had hoped. She worked first to David Hunt as Under-Secretary of State. A year later, in 1994, she was promoted to minister of state, working to Michael Portillo.

Widdecombe was responsible for training, but the economy was prospering, unemployment falling, and government measures like training councils had already been set up and were working to plan. She admits she was becoming frustrated: 'Of the three jobs I did in government, Employment was the least sharp. After a while I thought "What's this job about", no creativity.'

The scope for big measures was limited, but Widdecombe persevered, launching a campaign called 'Getting On' to persuade employers to take on older workers. 'There was increasing evidence that there was age discrimination in employment, in fact I think there probably still is. I know there still is. And we devised a campaign to try and persuade employers that older people were not a liability, they were actually an asset, because they had experience.' The campaign included a drive to find the oldest full-time employee in the country. The experience was enlightening: 'At the time I thought we would probably get somebody of 79, we might be lucky and get somebody of 80. A week later we had to say: nobody under 85 need apply for this. And in the end, the oldest worker we found was a 94 year old man who worked a six day week. We also found a woman of ninety three who worked a six day week and I still have contact with her from time to time. They got MBEs and they went on to Buckingham Palace. I look back to that with pleasure actually, it was a good time.'

Employment issues also thrust Widdecombe into the mire of 'political correctness', the bogey of left-wing lawyers, worthy do-gooders and some local councillors. For her, that was bad news. 'One thing I did not like about employment was the political correctness. The whole thing about 'rights', I found quite difficult.' Institutions like the Equal Opportunities Commission and women's groups would seek to make representations to the Minister about inequality at work, but Widdecombe could not hide her scepticism. 'I do think sometimes bodies like the Equal Opportunities Commission look around to find causes to justify their existence. There was a real cause in the mid-seventies when all this legislation was passed, both in terms of racial equality and women's equality, I think they were genuine issues. When I graduated in 1972, it was still perfectly lawful to offer two rates for the same job (one for a man and one for a woman).

'It was also lawful for people running flat agencies to discriminate against women; it was lawful for people recruiting for jobs, selling mortgages to say we don't deal with women. And I met that the whole time when I first graduated. It was blatant discrimination.'

But even earlier in her life, Ann had seen racial discrimination in action, and the event is etched on her memory. 'When I was a schoolgirl, my mother met me at Paddington and we went to lunch, at what were then 'the dining rooms' of Paddington station. We sat there and two black people came in and were turned away, on the grounds that they could not be served because they were black. My mother said, "I think we'll leave now", and we did. That sort of discrimination was perfectly lawful.'

Her conclusion: 'Those Commissioners had a real job to do in those early years. As that sort of prejudice has been overcome the really pressing nature of the job has declined, and that is when you start to look for reasons to be there. Obviously there is still some way to go but it's a very different world now".

Widdecombe had long had her eyes on working in the Home Office and in 1995, that aspiration was realised, when John Major moved her there to be Minister of State working for Michael Howard. She would have responsibility for the Prison Service and immigration. 'It was the first shuffle in which I was really pleased by the thing I'd been given. I had always wanted to go to the Home Office, the fact is I admired Michael Howard and I loved the jobs I was given.' His toughness and right wing set of beliefs suggested to her that he was someone she could work with.

However, that admiration would not last, and in due course the two would have a celebrated falling out. Widdecombe would now be known as a woman who did not like to be messed with. So Doris Karloff was born. Fleet Street had decided that Widdecombe was the new Dracula of Westminster.

The falling out with Michael Howard happened early in her time at the Home Office, although the public would not realise the extent of it until almost two years later. The trigger for the row, as Widdecombe expressed in her breath-taking speech in May 1997, was Michael Howard's speech to the House of Commons in October 1995, where he explained why he sacked the then director general of the prison service Derek Lewis. Howard said Lewis was ultimately responsible for operational matters, and so he should carry the can for a breakout from Parkhurst Prison on the Isle of Wight, and not the Home Secretary who was only responsible for broad policy matters. The matter was further complicated because Howard had earlier told Lewis to suspend the governor of Parkhurst, so breaking the supposed distinction between operational and policy responsibility made in his Commons speech.

Howard's wriggling and search for scapegoats created an unpleasantness and distance between the Home Secretary and the Home Office Minister that would rankle for 18 months, when both would be out of a government job following the May 1997 election. But Ann Widdecombe is anxious to correct the impression that she and Howard were at constant war following the incident. 'We did not have a continual war of attrition, we would not have lasted two years like that. Just as we have worked together in shadow cabinet, so we worked together in the Home Office. We are both grown ups, we wanted a Conservative victory, at times I wonder if some of our colleagues did, but we did. Perfectly possible to work with people you disagree with.' To prove the point she says she appointed the centrist MP Peter Luff to be her parliamentary private secretary.

The opening of the new Parliament in May 1997 was the moment Widdecombe chose to get off her chest a detailed account of her disagreement with Michael Howard. It was a particularly strategic time in the life of the post-landslide Conservative Party, as John Major had resigned and Michael Howard had put his hat into the ring as a contender for the vacant Conservative crown.

On the afternoon of 19 May 1997, a mere two weeks after the Labour victory, a packed House of Commons heard the former Minister at the Home Office deliver a set of remarks which she acknowledged at the beginning 'would be less than encouraging to her right hon and learned friend the Member for Folkestone and Hythe (Michael Howard).' She also asserted that she made the remarks 'with genuine sadness, and considerable reluctance But for my utter conviction of their rightness and of the imperative that lies behind them, I should not be making these remarks

21

at all.'

What followed was a defence of a Derek Lewis's period as director general of the prison service; a detailed examination of Michael Howard's explanations for the sacking of Derek Lewis; an analysis of the form of Howard's 'instruction', 'recommendation' or whatever to Lewis regarding his treatment of John Marriott, the governor of Parkhurst Prison. And finally, Ann Widdecombe made an outright condemnation of the character of her boss, whom she had once so respected. The fact that she stated the charges against him in unusually personal terms says much about the style and character of her politics. 'My right hon and learned friend has a problem,' she charged, 'in that his first reaction to attack is denial and refuge in semantic prestidigitation'. She further accused him of looking for scapegoats.

She concluded by saying that she had contemplated resignation at the time. But now she regretted her decision not to resign. She said the decision to make the speech required much soul-searching, but she made it 'in the interests of giving very belated justice to Mr Lewis, of giving some comfort to his wife Louise, who supported him faithfully.'

Two years later, Widdecombe said the decision not to resign had been taken to spare John Major's crisis-ridden administration yet another blow. The mention of Derek Lewis' wife in the Commons set-piece speech may seem curious, even irrelevant, were it not for some claims in the press that Derek Lewis had paid unusual attention to Ann Widdecombe, by sending her flowers. This caused much ribaldry and was read as mischievous spin-doctoring by members of the Howard camp. It was of course never taken seriously by Widdecombe and her supporters. That calumny amongst others may have been the explanation for the publication of a phrase uttered in private that she never later disowned. This attributed to Michael Howard 'something of the night'. The charge has remained to haunt the former Home Secretary. Its power lies in its vagueness said Widdecombe. 'I think the whole beauty of that phrase is that you're not quite sure what it means, and I'm not going to go into any more detail on that!' She merely adds that it was prompted by a particular event and set of feelings. 'It was an extremely specific attack, it wasn't about everything in general.'

The decision to make a speech that she knew would damage someone else's reputation so grievously came after much soul-searching and Widdecombe even consulted her priest before delivering it. When the Speaker called her to speak, she admits to feeling queasy, the only time in her career she has really felt nervous in such a situation. But as the speech progressed, and for once she had written down every word, she got the feeling she was doing the right thing. At the end, when she sat down, she 'felt a sense of peace.'

That was fine for her, of course, but she was still very con-cerned that the Party might bring their collective wrath down upon her for letting the side down. It turned out just the reverse. Her party appreciated her judgement, and the opprobrium she feared never materialised. She says: 'The great taboo in party politics is attacking someone on your own side. It is the great undone thing. I believed at the time that what I was doing would be hated by so many people. I was very apprehensive about it. I expected a hell of a time from my own party, and I didn't get it.'

Despite the prisons fracas, in the course of Widdecombe's two years at the Home Office she built up a reputation for toughness, at least the equal of Michael Howard. Two events confirmed this view. The first concerned her prison service role, and the second her work with the immigration service.

When Channel Four programme showed a pregnant woman prisoner manacled to a warder while in hospital, it was assumed that this was approved practice, and that she as prisons minister condoned it: not only that but chaining women in labour and childbirth. The media and the Labour Party rounded on her as a heartless harridan. The more malicious tabloids dubbed her with the name which has stuck, Doris Karloff.

Widdecombe rebuts the accusation as a calumny, and has

challenged it every time it was repeated in the press. She has won numerous apologies from newspapers as a result. She says the woman prisoner shown manacled in the film had only been put into hand-cuffs while she was outside the labour ward to have a cigarette. While she was in the ward, she had free movement without handcuffs or other restraint, and this was the policy.

'I have never defended—and it was never a policy—to secure women either in childbirth or indeed in labour. They were always secured between prison and hospital just as men are secured between prison and hospital. When you get to hospital and medical treatment starts you remove the restraints. I have never postulated in all my life that you should secure people in labour, that is a distortion which isn't borne out in the Hansard record. We have never had a policy of doing that, and we wouldn't do it.'

The claim that such policy was followed had actually arisen from an incident three months before she joined the Home Office when a woman gave birth in handcuffs. The former minister says this was over-zealousness by a prison officer as the female prisoner had previously attempted to escape in the course of an ante-natal appointment. 'There was an over zealous reaction to that. All that was settled and apologised for before I came in to the prison service. That incident and me were totally unrelated.' She also reaped some opprobrium for sanctioning the use of a ship as a floating prison, to relieve the much over-crowded prison service.

Immigration was an area where Widdecombe also took a tough stand, and where she identified herself clearly with the right wing of the Conservative Party. She cites the case of immigrants resisting deportation by taking refuge in a church. Her religious convictions were irrelevant to a potentially dangerous abuse of the law.

'I took a very tough line. My line was, 'we have a law', we have compassionate exceptions to that law, if you don't satisfy either the law or the compassionate grounds for exception, that's it. And once you make exceptions for people because they've done something unusual like hiding in a church, you simply create an atmosphere in which that is all people have got to do. So I actually took a very tough line.'

The need to crack down on illegal immigrants led Widdecombe into sanctioning some uncompromising police operations. 'We did on one occasion entice somebody out of a church; somebody went and banged on the door and said he was the Vicar, he was not the Vicar. But the chap came out quite voluntarily, there was no question of storming, nobody actually stormed the church; I might have done, if I'd had to. Unless every church in the country is going to be occupied by people seeking to evade the asylum laws, you've got to have a very clear line set. You have to make an example; you only ever have to do these things once to show that you will actually do it.'

Widdecombe had responsibility for asylum, and this took her into a number of controversial areas. 'I was deportations minister which meant I got all the rotten immigration cases right at the end of the line and some of the most controversial ones. Widdecombe took the initiative in seeking the deportation of the London-based Saudi dissident Al Mas'ari. But her compromise plan to have him sent to the island of Dominica was quashed by the courts.

The 1997 election was a shock to Widdecombe more by its scale than by outcome. The Conservative problem, she says simply, was that the party had won the previous four elections. The electorate wanted a change of faces, not policies. So when Labour took the Conservative agenda, the old hands were helpless. 'The election I think was unwinnable. It wasn't an easy night. The worst thing about that night was watching very close friends lose their seats, watching other close friends almost lose their seat by a whisker, not sure whether had had lost or not.' Among the friends she most missed after the election were Michael Portillo, David Hunt and Tony Newton.

Widdecombe was one of the first of the old ministerial team to bounce back from the jaws of defeat. She demonstrated in her platform speech to the party conference in 1998, when she stomped across the stage, spoke without notes, and brought disillusioned Tories to their feet, that she more than most understood what it meant to be opposition, and not in power. The rousing oratory rallied the hopelessly demoralised Conservative troops, her abomination of factionalism touched a cord in the hearts of Tories who did not understand the way the party had been splintered in the Major years.

Widdecombe would rather John Major had stayed as leader, and she was not prepared to jump straight onto William Hague's bandwagon. But she accepted the will of the party and vouched her loyalty to the new leader. Widdecombe spent a year on the back benches, and used the time to write a book and front a television programme. In May 1998, Hague offered her a job in the unfamiliar area of health, although her research for the Bow Group many years earlier had already indicated an interested in aspects of the hospital service.

It quickly became clear that Widdecombe would not be a slasher and burner of the NHS. The health service would be 'safe in her hands' she maintained. The priority would rather be finding new and probably private forms of finance to plug the holes left by the state provision. On taking up the role, she stated clearly and unequivocally: 'the Conservative Party has promised to increase annual expenditure in real terms on the Health Service'.

But Widdecombe also argued that 'it does not matter what the State spends on the health service, you cannot keep up with demand. Therefore you must get money in from elsewhere.' The British health service commands a smaller proportion of gross domestic product than medical facilities in equivalently developed countries, she said, and the logical response was to extend private participation. 'There should be no Berlin Wall between the private and public sectors'.

Two consequences flowed from this view. First, private insurance should be encouraged to cover health and she embarked on a study of a scheme offering employers tax incentives to take out health insurance for their workforces. Secondly, the private sector should make a greater contribution to the public area through extending the scope of the Private Finance Initiative.

Many proposals to stimulate incentives to take up private healthcare were initiated while Widdecombe was holding the shadow health brief. These included introducing tax incentives on health insurance. The underlying principle was that taxes on insurance should be regarded as 'obstacles'. She gave an example. 'Supposing you are an employer, you say everyone gets private health insurance from the director to the doorman. And the doorman says no thanks, I will have to pay tax on that as if it were income. I don't want that. I want more take home pay. I don't want this thing. The employer has to pay national insurance on this thing as though it were income. Those are the sorts of things I would call obstacles. I am not saying—and it is not Tory policy—that we will do away with all tax blocks on this type of thing. But we will look at the disincentives, and how much benefit would there be both to the individual and to the tax-payer if you removed some of those blocks, or if you introduced carrots.'

It was also asserted at the time that the Party was examining the possibility of reintroducing tax relief on insurance premiums for the elderly, removed by the present government. Those tax reliefs would have to be finely targeted. 'It is no good introducing tax reliefs to people like me who already take out private medicine insurance anyway. That is no good. If you are going to in to introduce tax relief you have got to encourage a significant proportion of people to take it up to have gained anything at all.'

PFI techniques were Widdecombe's preferred way of stimulating private sector investment in the hospital service. Her ministerial experience in the prison service, where PFI was used to fund entire prisons, enabled her to see how PFI principles could be used to fund expensive capital items in health, like scanners. If this equipment were used jointly by the private and public sectors, the public sector would also benefit.

'The one place where the PFI has been a big success is in the prison service. In the prison service, every new prison has been designed, constructed, financed and then managed by the private sector under contract to the home office. It is a total PFI and that is where the biggest successes have occurred. I am not suggesting that you go as far as that in the National Health Service over night. But what there is a huge gap waiting to be bridged between what we do in the Health Service which is buildings and a few little ancillary services, and what is done in the prison service.'

Private sector money will, according to the shadow Home Secretary, help to deal with the inequalities and inadequacies of healthcare rationing which she insists is endemic in the system and set to grow. 'I called rationing 'rationing'. But when I put a very simple question to the government, "is there or is there not rationing", the word came back no, just no. Not even a qualification. That as far as I am concerned is a lie. Until we admit rationing, we cannot start thinking about how we can minimise it. And if I am right, that rationing will increase unless we seek some exciting solution, the group of people who cannot afford the private sector and are in need of services or medicines not available in the public sector will grow.'

Ann Widdecombe's appointment as Shadow Home Secretary in 1999 (and her selection as Hague's stand-in over the summer break) has shown how her esteem has risen in Conservative ranks since the 1997 election. Privately many would also say that her straight-speaking over Michael Howard has done her career no disservice, although she would certainly rebut that as a motive for the extraordinary speech. She is unstinting in her loyalty to William Hague, whom she says is a fine orator, insightful and very patient. The widely-held contention that he is merely a stop-gap for the eventual return of Michael Portillo is rejected out of hand. 'Michael is not a king across the water,' she asserts, and the Conservative Party does not change its leaders as often as the media would like.

In her new post Widdecombe has taken on the twin roles of party spokesman for the media and Home Office policy think-tank. Indeed, her media appearances have so rattled the Labour Government that it is said to have instructed its dirty tricks department to target her.

As far as her policy-making role goes, Widdecombe is developing a prisons policy, much as she earlier developed a health policy, and along many of the same lines. 'I see some parallels between the police and health. Public expectation and demand are insuperably higher than the supply of available manpower and money. I have very strong views on how prisons should be managed. Prison days should be constructed so that you maximise the chance of people leaving prison equipped to lead a law abiding life. If you don't do that you don't protect the public.'

As to the next election, Ann Widdecombe must believe that the Conservatives will win. But in the unfortunate event of the Conservatives losing, but 'losing well', she believes William Hague will survive as leader. On that basis, Hague will have a very loyal lieutenant in Ann Widdecombe. Her ambition in waiting patiently by his side will only be realised with the election of a new Conservative Government. There, her preferred role would be Home Secretary.

In the meantime, Ann's role is to rouse the troops, boost morale and castigate the doubting Thomases. The Labour Party will grow increasingly to hate her. More importantly, she will make sure they fear her.

Excellence in Education

In 1969 Ann Widdecombe left the University of Birmingham with a degree in Latin and went to Oxford ostensibly to read Politics, Philosophy and Economics but in reality to prepare for the political career she was now resolved on. She joined the Oxford Union and became Secretary and Treasurer. While Secretary she appeared in her first televised debate opposing the motion that 'equality is more important than excellence in education'. The President of the Union was then Sue Richards, now Sue Kramer the Liberal Democrat candidate for Mayor of London. The then Labour ministers Dick Crossman and Shirley Williams spoke in favour of the motion and Norman St. John Stevas and Professor Cox spoke against. One of the undergraduates mentioned, Julian Priestly, subsequently fought for Labour against Dr. David Owen at Devonport in the 1983 General Election. Ann Widdecombe was the Conservative candidate for that seat at the same time.

* * *

Madam President, Ma'am. The Treasurer, in his proposition speech, made an attack on the public schools as the ultimate in segregation and in putting excellence ahead of equality. Now it is not the contention of this side of the House tonight that excellence and equality must be mutually exclusive but simply that, given our present system of education, they do not often co-exist side by side; that there are times when we have to make a choice between excellence and equality and that when we have to make that choice, we should decide in favour of excellence.

I am not against a utopia in which everybody has an equally excellent education but what I am saying is that in working towards the realisation of that ideal, we do have to make choices along the way and this is what perhaps has been most neglected in argument tonight: that there do have to be choices. My contention is that we should choose excellence. Let me first turn to Public Schools which have been much maligned in practically all the speeches on the proposition side tonight. The Honourable proposer gave a list of their advantages and their superior standards which any advocate of the public school system would have been proud to have compiled. And he then grumbles that there is greater confidence in the products of public schools. Well that confidence stems from those superior standards as much as from social attitudes.

Now, it is a scandal - and undoubtedly a scandal - that there is the dichotomy of standards which exists between this country's private system of education and its State system, but that dichotomy does exist and the individual should therefore be free to choose between them where he is able. It is a nonsense to say that when the State cannot provide - or does not provide - the standards which the Public Schools provide we should therefore deprive people of being able to choose against the State and being able to choose a better education for their children.

Now I am not necessarily in favour of segregation at 11. I am in favour of segregation - not necessarily at 11, which I think is a particular of the argument we are having, rather than the essence of it. The system which has been working in this country for some time of segregating children - currently at 11 - has produced some quite good results. Mrs Shirley Williams spoke of the higher numbers entering the universities, the higher numbers entering the teacher training colleges. Is this a product of a wholly comprehensive system? No. It is the product of a system which has, for a long time, been segregating at 11.

In a very airy-fairy fashion, Mr Priestley dismissed the odd person who failed the 11 plus and then got on in life. He seems to think it's a very odd occurrence indeed. In fact, although I wouldn't exactly say it was common, it happened a lot. I am one of the products you see before you tonight.

Neither do I think that the comprehensive system, which has been much extolled tonight, will do away with the effects of segregation. We know that there are social attitudes which seem to hold that the child who is bright is somehow a superior child - is a child more worthy of respect - and that the children who are less able academically, and I stress academically, are something to be looked down upon. Nobody probably feels this more than the children concerned, so one of the worst things that you can do is to put a child who feels that attitude and who knows that he isn't academically capable - into a school side by side with a child who is bright, who is destined for Oxford, for Cambridge, for wherever else. That is one of the worst ways in which to intensify those social attitudes.

In a grammar school, certainly, you have your C-stream along with the very bright coming out of your A-stream, but even the C stream are able. But, if you have a comprehensive school - even if it is streamed, which is by no means always the case, with abilities ranging from people who are very bright indeed to people who, academically speaking, are not bright at all, I maintain that it is grossly unfair on those children who are poor performers. Whereas segregate them - give them an education suited to their particular needs and they will find their role in society - they will find a purpose to education.

Now, I don't say decide irrevocably at 11 who is bright and who isn't bright but I do say that somewhere along the line you have got to segregate those who need one kind of education and those who need another - not necessarily inferior - but a very different sort of education. Perhaps segregation at 11 does mean that those children whose qualities - like Professor Cox - emerge early are given a lot of preference but equally so, if we have segregation later on, we have generally reached a stage where the potential of children is pretty clear. It is true there are a lot of children who, for some reason or other, seem to realise much greater achievements between the ages of 11 and 13 than they have before 11. I suppose if the line had to be drawn somewhere on segregation, I would say perhaps 13 , but I do believe that the greatest error that society can commit is to say that because we need special teaching for our less bright children - and we certainly do - that therefore we should start pouring scorn on those who say that children with immense potential should have the best possible, excellent education.

Society needs the best from everyone and the way for each to give his best is to be well taught according to his needs. Therefore excellence must not be sacrificed to equality.

Capital Punishment

Ann Widdecombe is a firm believer in Capital Punishment being available to the courts. She debated the subject first at the Oxford Union and then in 1978 she had an amendment selected at Party Conference, welcoming the Conservative commitment to a parliamentary debate and free vote on reintroducing the death penalty. Her arguments were as follows:

* * *

In moving this amendment I am the first to acknowledge that we would all probably prefer to do without capital punishment, to have fewer prisons and fewer people in those prisons. It is right that a civilised society should have those aspirations but they can only be realised as crime is reduced. We can not do without appropriate penalties as long as crime is rife.

It was right that in 1965 we tried to do without Capital Punishment but the effects of that experiment should have led us to restore—not abolish permanently—the supreme penalty when the period of experimental abolition was over.

During those five years of so called experimental abolition the capital murder rate rose by a staggering 125%. This proves beyond all reasonable doubt that the death penalty acted as a deterrent and saved innocent life. During the same period there was a fourfold increase in murders involving shooting, thus demonstrating equally conclusively that the oft made claim that older criminals were wont to frisk younger ones to make sure they were not carrying firearms is fact not fiction. Similarly murder committed in the course of theft rose threefold.

These figures can not be ignored. They mean that the lifting of a serious deterrent has unleashed a huge increase not only in murder but in violent crime. My view is that we now have a duty to restore the death penalty. I would prefer that it should be available for all premeditated murder but if the problem of definition should prove too hard, then at least it must be applicable to the murder of prison officers, police officers, terrorist murders and all murder committed in the course of armed robbery.

I know that it is often contended that to hang a terrorist is to create a martyr but I take the view that every terrorist in prison is a focus for further outrage and atrocity.

I do not say bring back capital punishment for ever. There may well come a time when we want once more to try and do without it but the current experiment has failed. We should admit that and act accordingly.

The above is not a word for word transcript of Ann's speech. Sadly no such document exists but it is a distillation of her many speeches and comments on this issue and press reporting at the time.

Maiden Speech

In 1982 Ann Widdecombe helped Olga Maitland to found Women and Families for Defence, an organisation set up to counter the activities of the Greenham Common Women. The issue of nuclear arms played a major role in the 1983 General Election and was still a hot potato when Ann Widdecombe was elected to Parliament in June 1987. In October that year she maid her maiden speech in a debate on the Defence Estimates. Labour were at that time still opposed to Britain having either Trident or Cruise Missiles.

* * *

I am grateful for the opportunity to make my first speech in the House in this important debate. In doing so, I pay tribute to my distinguished predecessor, Sir John Wells, who served the constituency with dedication and distinction for 28 years. His period of service will be remembered by his former constituents with respect and affection, as I am sure it will also be remembered by Members of the House. He earned respect for his exemplary chairmanship of many important parliamentary Committees and affection for the colourful way in which he sometimes drew attention to the needs of his constituents. On one occasion, he arrived for the day's business on a horse. On another, he enlivened proceedings in the Chamber by eating an apple - a Kentish apple, of course - during the debate. I hope to follow his example in dedicating myself to the service of my constituents, but I shall not be eating any apples in the Chamber, as history attests rather strongly to the unfortunate results of ladies eating apples when they should not.

My constituency has suffered badly from the recent wind storms. As a horticulturist, Sir John Wells would have understood all too well the misery and devastation suffered by many farmers, especially the fruit farmers whose industry takes up such a large part of the constituency that I have the honour to serve. I hope that the Government will see fit to provide some compensation, in however cautious and measured a way, to those who have lost their livelihood not just in the immediate term but for years to come, because it will be some time before replanted trees can be expected to produce crops which will generate income.

Leaving the country areas for the town of Maidstone, I am proud to have in that town concrete and tangible evidence of the Government's firm commitment to the National Health Service in the shape of a large new modern hospital. I regret to tell the House, however, that, due to inequitable distribution of funds by the South East Thames regional health authority, that hospital is not being used as fully or as beneficially as it should be. On an appropriate future occasion, I hope to draw attention to the difficulties experienced by my constituents as a result of that inequitable distribution of funds.

I address myself to the debate and to the Opposition amendments in the sure knowledge that I address myself to a subject of the utmost importance and interest to constituents. I begin by congratulating the Government on the Defence Estimates and particularly on the sound basis on which they have drawn up plans for the nation's security. I believe that the people of Britain will draw great comfort and reassurance from the fact that they are governed by a party which is wholly committed to an effective nuclear deterrent.

I spent many hours yesterday and some today listening to Opposition Members decrying the Trident programme. I thought that they had been sufficiently effectively answered yesterday, but today we have heard the same tired arguments, based on the same flawed logic. Both their amendments and in the many distinguished speeches that we have heard, the Opposition have claimed that the Trident programme is undesirable because it eats into conventional defence expenditure. There is a severe absence of logic in that statement. It is true that if we did not spend the money on Trident we could use it to purchase conventional weapons or, indeed, anything we liked - sacks of potatoes, biros, pounds of butter, whatever. If we are to spend Trident money on something other than Trident, we must ask ourselves whether the optional thing that we are purchasing is capable of doing the job of trident. If it is not capable of doing that job and fulfilling the aims of Trident, it does not matter that we could buy it with Trident money. It is totally irrelevant

The sole objective of Trident is to deter a potentially hostile force from launching a nuclear attack on this country, or to deter a hostile force with overwhelmingly superior conventional forces from attempting to use this superiority to launch a conventional attack. Therefore, if we are to give up Trident to buy conventional weapons we must demand that those weapons constitute an equally effective deterrent.

The statement on the Defence estimates suggests that if we devote all the Trident money to conventional weapons, we might be able to buy and maintain 300 tanks for an armoured division. I am sure that it is very laudable and worthy to buy 300 tanks for an armoured division but, when the Warsaw pact countries have a superiority of 30,000 tanks, it will not be a very effective deterrent. We can do the same arithmetical exercise for artillery, where we are outnumbered by 3:1, and in anti-tank guided weapons by 1.6:1. We can continue that exercise, but we shall not end up with a replacement that serves the same aim as Trident. We shall simply replace something designed to do one job with something designed to do a totally different job.

Opposition Members were not terribly kind to the Government last night when summing up. The hon. Member for Knowsley, South (Mr. Hughes) said that he would not award a CSE pass to the Government for the reasoning behind their Defence Estimates but, after listening yesterday and for several hours today to the Opposition, I do not believe that they have reached a standard of elementary logic which would get them through the 11-plus. Perhaps that is why they have such an antipathy towards that examination, My nephews and niece at the age of eight or nine, let alone 11 could have told Opposition Members that, if they are given the bus fare to get home and they spend it on a taxi ride, they will not get the same value because the taxi will take them only a few yards.

If we spend the Trident money on 300 tanks or whatever - frigates are much beloved of the opposition - we shall find that we have gone not even a few yards or feet but only a few inches towards an effective deterrent, whereas Trident would do the entire job, so the logic is flawed. If we all took to the hills - as the Opposition came perilously close to suggesting not long ago - and invested our Trident money in bows and arrows, those bows and arrows might outnumber those of the Warsaw pact countries but would be about as useful as some of the arguments put forward by the Opposition.

Opposition Members are trying to have it all ways when they argue that, if we are to have an independent deterrent, it must be truly independent. I am not quite sure what Opposition Members stand for. The distinguished and right hon. Member for Leeds, East (Mr. Healey) said that we do not have a truly independent deterrent because the Americans will do the servicing. We said very clearly - I am sorry that the Opposition did not understand the point - that we shall always have control over some of the missiles. Does the right hon. Gentleman seriously believe that, when he sends a suit to the cleaners, he has no clothes at all and must come into the Chamber in a state of sartorial dilapidation because he has no suit?

Finally, in desperation, Opposition Members decided to try to claim that the conventional imbalance was a figment of the Government's imagination, that it did not exist, and in support of that they triumphantly produced a document brought out by the International Institute for Strategic Studies and quoted it with the reverence normally reserved for Holy Writ. They said, "Look, this says something entirely different." I have read that document and I find that within its figures there is ample evidence, which is clearly set out and not at all disguised, that the Warsaw pact enjoys an overwhelming numerical superiority of conventional weapons. I commend page 226 to the Opposition for further study. They may not have got that far.

The amendment submitted in the name of the Leader of the Opposition is serious, because it exhorts the Government to take a headlong flight to abandon and abolish all battlefield nuclear weapons simultaneously with reductions on the conventional side. That is simply and solely the wrong timing. There must be no further reductions beyond the INIF treaty agreements. There must be no further reductions in nuclear weapons until such time as the conventional imbalance - whether one believes the Government's document or the IISS document - is eliminated.

In that context, I should like to ask my hon. Friend the Minister for reassurance later. It is said that the statement on the Defence Estimates was drawn up at a time when the finer ramifications of the INF proposals, particularly the inclusion of shorter-range intermediate missiles, had not been fully understood. Such are the massive implications for our conventional spending, not only for Britain, which already spends the third highest percentage of gross domestic product in NATO on defence, but for all our NATO partners, that we should be assured that not only will there be no simultaneous negotiations for the reduction of battlefield nuclear weapons, but that there will be a good long cool gap before any agreement that we may reach on conventional weapons while we assess the implications.

So desperate were the anti-Trident Opposition that they said that there was supposed to be an escalation of the arms race. One sees such words in the amendments. That is interesting. An arms race implies that each side is trying to keep up with the other, but as I read it, the number of warheads on Trident is a lower proportion of Warsaw warheads than Polaris was when we first had it. So that is not an escalation.

The Opposition used the worn-out argument that because the warheads were independently targeted, we had increased our numbers. However, if one is talking about an arms race, one must also look at what the other side is doing. Surely it is only prudent, when designing a system, to say that if one ever reached the highly undesirable state when one needed to increase one's warheads, one should have the system to make that possible. The cost of the Chevaline operation that was forced upon the Labour Government can be interpreted as the cost of not having sufficient forward defence planning at the time of procurement.

I regret that in this, my first speech in the House, I have had to devote so much time to the wild and woolly arguments of the Opposition. I am also rather surprised that they are still putting forward in the House the Alice-in-Wonderland reasoning that lost them the June election. I say to them: Come back from Wonderland. Do not go through the looking glass with Alice. Instead, stay in front of the looking glass and take a good long look. Do the Opposition's policies reflect public opinion? No. But more importantly, do their policies have any bearing on the real world? Surely the answer must still be no. Thus the Opposition should stand at that looking glass and look in. But my belief is that the general public, as exhibited in poll after poll, have reason to be thankful and grateful to the Government who have drawn up their plans on a sound and effective deterrent rather than being able to offer no strategy and no alternative.

1987

Abortion

*Before entering Parliament Ann Widdecombe had been a vigor-
ous opponent of abortion, a member of the Society for the
Protection of Unborn Children and had debated the issue at both
Birmingham and Oxford Universities. When she converted to
Catholicism in 1993 she said that Rome's stand on abortion was
one of the factors which drew her to that Church. Ann was therefore delighted when in 1987, the year she entered Parliament,
David Alton the Liberal MP for Liverpool Mossley Hill, introduced
a Bill to make abortion after the eighteenth week illegal. She
spoke during the course of the Second Reading Debate.*

* * *

I support the Bill. I am motivated by the fact that it endeavours to
do what the 1967 Act lamentably failed to achieve. It tries to
define where life starts, and the rights of one individual over the
life of another.

We all accept that if someone is born perfectly healthy and
then, through illness or a major accident, becomes grossly handicapped, that person still has the right to live and is classified as
a separate human being with full civil rights. We all accept that if
a child is damaged because something goes wrong at birth, such

as oxygen failure, that child is a human being with fully established civil rights, and has the right to live, no matter how handicapped.

We do not allow a woman to choose whether to continue a pregnancy when she is more than 28 weeks pregnant. We already say that there must be some restriction of one individual's right of determination over another's right to live. I support the Bill because it asks whether we have got it right (the current restrictions) and if not why not and what should be the correct limit.

The Bill has been described by various hon. Members who oppose it as muddled. I maintain strongly that the 1967 Act was a muddle. The 1967 Act said that what is in the womb is not life because a woman has a right of abortion under certain loose circumstances. It also said that perhaps it is life, and perhaps we should protect it, so we shall define the circumstances in which a woman can have an abortion, be they ever so loose. It fudged the issue. We must decide when life is life and must be fully and absolutely respected, as hon. Members would respect each other's lives. It has been widely accepted that babies survive at 24 weeks, although it would be conceded by my hon. Friends, that it is a massive struggle and only a minority survive, but they survive.

I find it deeply objectionable - I will not use a pejorative word such as obscene - that we have a law that permits two babies to leave their mother's womb at 24 weeks; one is cherished while its life is fought over, and all the medical resources in the country are poured into saving it and its parents desperately want it to live, while the other is wilfully destroyed, being - taken from its mother's womb unnaturally at the same age. I find that impossible to accept as a mark of a civilised society.

I find it unacceptable that we should have those two completely separate attitudes towards a child of the same age. It is even reflected in our language. I have never heard a woman who lost a baby prematurely say that she lost her foetus; she says she has lost her baby. Yet when we decide that we will wilfully destroy a 24-week-old baby, we call it a foetus. That is a dual standard. I am concerned that the Abortion Act 1967 legislated for that standard, and I want to see a revision.

Where do we draw the line? Is it at the presently recorded lowest survival rate of 24 weeks for permanent survival and 23 weeks for temporary survival, or at the point where we think medical science will move in the foreseeable future, or do we recognise as life the time when a child is fully formed, is sentient and can feel pain and react to stimuli? We have all reached different decisions of conscience. The Bill is a valid attempt to set down a line, and I support the line that the Bill has set down.

I recognise fully that other hon. Members have different opinions. For the sake of the 92 per cent of healthy children who are aborted over the age of 18 weeks I would not stick doctrinally to a position where the exceptions were so narrow that the Bill would be lost through that. I would rather compromise, even if it goes against what I personally believe, in order to save that 92 per cent. I am sorry that my hon. Friend the Member for Berkshire, East (Mr. MacKay) is not here to hear me say this, because his major concern was that he did not trust the hon. Member for Liverpool, Mossley Hill (Mr. Alton) to put together a Committee that would be capable of absorbing that compromise. As an anti-abortionist, I will face that compromise if by doing so I can save unborn life and many of my hon. Friends would take that view. [1]

The same goes for the line we draw. To be perfectly honest, I would draw the line below the one that the hon. Member for Mossley Hill has drawn, but if in order to save a certain proportion of unborn life I must accept a slightly higher line, I will, with reluctance, accept that line. All that I ask is that this important Bill which fills a gap that the 1967 Act left unaddressed and attempts to define the rights of individuals who cannot speak for themselves, should have a chance to be fully examined and to return to the House for final approval or disapproval. I would say to my hon. Friend the Member for Berkshire, East: let us not shut the door this morning This matter is too important. We must keep the door open because what finally emerges will be a wise, humane and civilised Bill; and the present legislation fulfils non of those criteria.

Footnote: There was a strong body of opinion arguing that handicapped children should be exempted from the proposed 18 week limit. Figures showed that only 8% of those aborted after the eighteenth week were handicapped. Pro Lifers were divided over whether to resist any exemptions to the eighteenth week limit and thereby risk losing the Bill or as Ann Widdecombe was indicating here to build in an exemption for serious handicap.

1988

The Channel Tunnel

In 1988 British Rail put forward four possible routes for a high speed link from the Channel Tunnel to London. All the routes encompassed devastation to countryside and villages and Kent MPs began a fight that was to last for years. Ann Widdecombe raised a debate on compensation for the thousands affected. She also vigorously and successfully opposed "Route 3", which would have run across the Weald and her Constituency.

* * *

I am grateful for this opportunity to raise the issue of compensation for people who will be affected by the proposed high-speed rail link between the Channel Tunnel and London, running through Kent. I sincerely hope that, in the event, my constituents will not be affected.

British Rail has proposed four routes for the high-speed railway. The fourth has been dropped as being too costly and taking too long to construct. One of the three remaining routes will affect my constituents very badly. The other two give rise to points that I am raising on behalf of the people of Kent generally, rather than of my constituents alone.

Routes one or two should be chosen. I have to agree with the Chairman of Eurotunnel, Alistair Morton, who says that he can see no good reason why we are even still considering route three. Whichever route is chosen will cause problems for the people of Kent and there are objections to be advanced against all three. Therefore we must consider whether there are any positive reasons for accepting any of the routes and whether they provide any benefit for the people of Kent.

The prospects with routes one and two are quite good. First, there is the possibility of an economic boost for the Medway, which traditionally has been the poorer part of Kent. Secondly, there is the possibility of an improved rail commuter service, of a parkway at Maidstone, and, not least, of a link with the north through King's Cross. That must surely play a fairly major part in British Rail's long-term plans.

More important, all Kent is up in arms over the environmental threat from the high-speed railway. Routes one or two could probably be put through tunnels, and certainly through cuttings, for much of their length. Route three runs across the Weald with its wet clay soil, and the line would have to be raised. As such, it would be unsightly and noisy and the environmental damage would be very much greater than from routes one and two. Thus there is no advantage in it, especially as it would be slower than route one, and on this high-speed link the faster the service the higher the revenue for British Rail, and more costly than route two. I see no reason why we are still considering it and why my constituents cannot be immediately relieved of their fear, their worry and the planning blight that is caused by this wholly pointless route. Alistair Morton can see no point in it, nor can British Rail, and nor can the people of Kent.

Enormous questions are raised about compensation for people along the chosen route. I have made available in advance the points that I shall raise both with the Minister and British Rail in the hope that I shall obtain some fairly clear and definite answers, at least where possible. The issues are complex. We have built no new railways since the turn of the century and our compensation laws are therefore inadequate and in a mess. The laws that apply to motorways do not apply in the same way to railways, which leaves far too little protection for Kent constituents who are affected by the new project.

So worried are my constituents that they have formed a campaign to save the heart of Kent - the Weald, Bourne valley and the villages that will be destroyed should route three be chosen. The village of Collier Street will become completely unrecognisable. Headcorn and Staplehurst will be sandwiched between two railway lines and a naturally beautiful part of Kent will be destroyed. Those are just some of the disadvantages.

It has been suggested that the building of a high-speed rail link will mean also a more intensive use of existing track, perhaps to carry more freight or perhaps to cope with the extra custom that British Rail expects. Residents near a railway line that carries no traffic between 11.30 pm and 6 am may sleep, undisturbed throughout the night. But if the line is used more intensively, with trains running through the night, no statutory compensation is provided for the people who suffer from the consequent noise. Compensation, would, however, have been payable when the line was built. Thousands of people in Kent will be affected if there is, as is generally projected, an intensification of use. I should like to hear some solid proposals for helping those people.

I do not join in the general bashing of British Rail that has been prevalent recently. British Rail had a hopeless task. It had to produce four hideous propositions, take them into the heart of Kent and sell them to people who were to be affected by them. Inevitably, it has been castigated for mistakes which it undoubtedly made. The people trying to sell the proposals were not official public relations men but British Rail officials. They did a good job, and are, continuing to do so, under difficult circumstances.

I am extremely grateful to British Rail for agreeing to make ex gratia payments to some of my constituents. Those payments must be ex gratia because, by law, British Rail is not obliged to provide compensation to persons affected by the route until the Bill needed to authorise the scheme receives Royal Assent. In the ordinary course of events, given that the project will probably proceed through Parliament under the auspices of a Private Bill, and as we have yet to have decisions from Kent County Council and British Rail, and they will have to wait for the matter to come before Parliament, it could be two years before that Royal Assent is granted.

However, British Rail has recognised the practical difficulties, one of which has already affected dozens of my constituents. People who had started to sell their houses before the routes were announced believed that the sales would go through. They therefore entered into commitments to buy elsewhere, sometimes in a completely different part of the country, to accommodate job moves and so on. When the routes were published the purchasers of their properties backed out. The vendors were stuck without compensation until Royal Assent. However, British Rail very properly agreed to make ex gratia payments to them to ease their financial burden. That is all very well for the people who had already started the sale process, but the position between now and Royal Assent of those hundreds of people who have not started the sale process but who will want, for perfectly genuine reasons, to sell their houses, is not clear.

British Rail has promised a package of assistance, before the route is chosen. Again I offer my thanks.

However, it is wholly unacceptable that there is no proper legal provision or guidance about how people should be treated in those circumstances. For example, I understand that in some EEC countries when railway disturbance is caused, not only is the property bought, as it would be here, through compulsory purchase, but a disturbance premium is paid in addition. Will our constituents get a disturbance premium, or will they merely get the compulsory purchase value? How will the value be determined? The market value of houses in Kent is extremely high. Once the chosen route is announced, the market value of the houses on it will decline. Will compensation be payable at the current market value, or at the prevailing market value when my constituents finally sell?

Agricultural land gives rise to many other problems. Whatever route is chosen, some farmers' land will obviously be required. Will they simply be compensated for the price of the land, or will the compensation also reflect the loss of income from that land? If they move the activities on that land elsewhere on the farm, it will take many years before the new location becomes income bearing. Will they be compensated for that? How will compensation be assessed when the land is purchased? Will it be based on agricultural land prices, which are not wonderful, or on development land prices, which, in the south-east, are? May we be told now, or do my constituents have to worry for a further two years about the basis of compensation?

Then there are those who fall outside the compulsory purchase bracket, but who will still be mightily affected by the railway. Again, that will apply no matter which route is chosen. My right hon. Friend the Member for Tonbridge and Malling (Sir John Stanley), who is here, is one of those hon. Members who are extremely worried about the plight of their constituents. There is a law on injurious affection, which I am informed has nothing to do with unfortunate love affairs, but is about being affected by noise, unsightliness or other such factors. That law was never designed to cover the impact of a railway.

Believe it or not, there is no statutory maximum noise limit on railways. There is a noise level above which compensation must be paid and noise bafflement measures must be taken, but a railway may emit any amount of noise. If this project leads to increased railway activity, there will be a fantastic increase also in noise. The people affected do not know what compensation they would get. There is no defined corridor within which it will be paid. Will it be paid to people who live within 200 yards of the railway, or within 400 yards? Will it depend on whether there are cuttings or embankments? Will it be measured with a noise meter?

Nobody appears to know.

Will people get money if they find that their living conditions become intolerable? Will they simply be given double glazing and told to get on with it? Will any account be taken of the complete destruction of a beautiful part of the country and of such views as our constituents may have enjoyed in the past? How exactly will the injurious affection law be applied?

It is easy to concentrate solely on residential properties, and most of the pronouncements from British Rail have been in respect of such properties and, very occasionally, of agricultural holdings. However, another class of person will be badly affected by the railway - the business man, particularly, the small business man.

I am beginning to receive quite a few letters from such people - one is in the constituency of my right hon. Friend the Member for Tonbridge and Malling - are losing orders because of the railway. Home improvement firms are particularly affected. They have had orders to build conservatories, for example, but suddenly their customers, believing that they might lose their properties, have cancelled those orders. The problem applies to people selling all sorts of goods and services in the affected areas. Will such people be compensated for loss of income? How long will they have to wait? Will they have gone into liquidation by the time any compensation is proposed? What will be done for businesses?

It is difficult to produce a full package of measures to deal with a completely new set of circumstances, but surely it was realised that the day would inevitably come when a new railway track would have be built. It must have been realised that we could not go on forever without any expansion of the rail network. It must have been clear that any major railway construction project would have presented complex and manifold problems. However, insufficient thought was given before the proposals were announced to ensuring that the necessary laws were on the statute book or that British Rail, as a nationalised industry, was given firm guidance.

There are many points that I have not raised, partly because time will not allow and partly because they are so numerous that I would not know where to begin. However, I can assure my hon. Friend the Minister that I have received thousands of letters, the vast bulk of which is against route three. Many of those letters contain heart-rending pleas from my constituents who are suffering personally as a result of the railway line.

To those people the choice of route, the method of calculating the compensation, and the permitted noise levels are personal, not academic, matters. Whichever route is chosen, constituents somewhere will be affected. However, wherever they are, the compensation laws that will cover them are in a mess. Ad hoc and emergency provision and ex gratia payments are not enough. We need a complete and utter overhaul of our compensation laws.

Footnote: In the end Route 2 was chosen.

The Preservation of Church Treasures

In July 1990 the House of Commons debated the preservation of Church treasures: cathedrals, silver, art and architecture. The debate took place in the early hours of the morning. Ann Widdecombe entered the Chamber and made a speech consisting of one line - a reference to a Biblical text.

Matthew chapter 6, verses 19 and 20.

There was a frantic consultation on both front benches and a Bible was sent for. The passage to which Miss Widdecombe referred reads "Lay not up for yourselves Treasure on this earth where the moth and the rust doth corrupt".

NOVEMBER 1992

A Letter to the Archbishop of Canterbury

In November 1992 the Church of England voted to ordain women as priests. A massive row ensued with several hundred clergy and a few thousand laity leaving. Most subsequently became Roman Catholics. With the row at its height Ann Widdecombe wrote an open letter to the Archbishop of Canterbury which was published by the Guardian on 26 January 1993. She became a Roman Catholic three months later.

* * *

"Be of good comfort Master Ridley... We shall this day light such a candle by God's grace in England as shall never be put out."

You will recognise the quote - those were the words of Hugh Latimer as he and a fellow bishop of the Church of England died for their faith in the flames nearly 400 years ago. If I had to give a graphic illustration of the present day Church of England it would be a picture of you and some of your fellow bishops determinedly puffing at that precious candle in an attempt to extinguish it altogether and bring to ashes Latimer's vision

Of course most of it isn't your fault - the rot had set in long before you came to Canterbury. I don't mean the modernisation of the Book of Common Prayer (although I think Cranmer had a better touch), nor modern hymns (I'm a great fan of Graham Kendrick), nor clapping in Church (Christians should be joyful), nor any other superficial change in our mode of worship. Whatever my personal preferences may be one cannot expect the language of the Church to stand still. No, I am talking about faith itself.

Montefiore questions the sexuality of Christ and is made a bishop before most of us have finished blinking in astonishment. Jenkins questions such fundamental articles of creed as the resurrection and the virgin birth and becomes Bishop of Durham. I haven't heard that they have abandoned the creed at Durham, so presumably either their bishop refrains from joining in or he says that which he is not sure he believes.

On a still day you can almost hear the laughter from the headquarters of perdition. These days they can't hold their tridents straight for mirth—mirth only equalled by that of church spokesmen when a thunderbolt struck York Minster shortly after the consecration of the Bishop of Durham and some God-fearing soul actually suggested that the Deity might be venturing an opinion. The Deity, their laughter seemed to suggest, wouldn't have the cheek.

It would be wrong to say the Church doesn't enter the great moral debates of our time. The Archbishop of York gave a major lead in favour of experiments on human embryos and is presumably proud of our brave new world in which reputable organisations now openly canvass licences to practise eugenics and question the right of the prematurely born to medical care.

So now we come to your time, Your Grace. I don't know whether to laugh or cry when I think how delighted I was at your appointment. Here was a man who believed in the sanctity of marriage and of unborn life, who believed in personal responsibility, who upheld traditional moral values, who was not ashamed to speak of a Jesus movement. I was at Canterbury for your enthronement and thought the Church was entering a period of spiritual renewal. Instead it was entering terminal decline.

This is not the place to rehearse again the theological arguments against the ordination of priestesses. It is the effects of the synod vote we must look at now - a vote which resulted in no small measure from the lead you gave.

I wonder if even now you appreciate the extent of the rift you have caused. Clergy and Laity will leave. Others will stay demanding arrangements for episcopal oversight which make a nonsense of Church unity. Others still will accept the situation until confronted with a Priestess as a candidate for their parish.

If Graham Leonard's approaches to Rome succeed, the Anglo-Catholic wing could desert on mass. I'm not talking idly. I received hundreds of letters after I left the Church saying just that. And your response to all this? Utter incomprehension that any one could disagree with you, or if someone did, that such a person could have the courage to act on such convictions.

As if the collapse of faith and now schism itself were not enough the Archbishop of York this weekend effectively proposed the ultimate disestablishment of the Church by suggesting that as we now live in a multi-faith society Prince Charles should not swear to uphold the Church of England when he succeeds the throne. I admire the Archbishop's faith that there will still be anything recognisable as the Church of England by the time of Charles III. If this suggestion came from a Labour MP it would be understandable. That it comes from the second most senior bishop in the Church of England can only lead one to conclude that either the church is run by lemmings in episcopal robes or else by ostriches with their heads stuck in the sands of eternal compromise.

If Prince Charles is to be head of the Church of England he must obviously uphold it. Anyone who has followed the events of recent weeks must conclude that damage to both monarchy and church has been of such an order of magnitude that they are both struggling for survival. It is scarcely the time to propose a separation of the ways but rather they must seem to strengthen each other.

The Archbishop's statement was of course an attempt to make the Church all things to all men of all faiths, but that is to confuse tolerance and respect of other creeds with the surrender of one's own. It is a confusion which has characterised too many of the Church's pronouncements in recent years.

So will you rebuke the Archbishop your Grace? Will you make it clear that you see an established place for the Church of England in the affairs of England and that you expect both Monarch and subjects to uphold it? Perhaps you can make it clear to some of the other bishops that you expect them to uphold the creed?

As you know I left the Church of England on November 11 and am in conversation with Westminster Cathedral. One of their practices which I've never been keen on is invoking the saints but if I were to do so I would invoke one not in their recognised list and the conversation might go like this:

"I'm sorry Hugh Latimer, I can't stay in your Church."

"Be of good comfort, Miss Ann. One day by God's grace the candle shall be rekindled and as I was remarking to Master Ridley at harps this morning I think we ought to start praying for the success of the Pope..."

Yours, sadly but with prayers
Ann Widdecombe

1993

The Ordination of Women

Nearly a year after the Church of England decided to ordain women as priests the House of Commons debated the measure in order to pass it into law. The debate produced two curiosities : Ann Widdecombe who was then a junior Employment minister and John Gummer who was in the Cabinet spoke from the back-benches and a host of Catholics, Jews, Agnostics and atheists filled the lobbies for the vote, causing some comment on the continuing relevance of an Established Church.

* * *

First, I congratulate my right hon. Friend the Member for Selby (Michael Alison) on the extremely comprehensive and moderate way in which he introduced the Measures, which I believe will have won the respect even of those who profoundly disagree with the reasons that he advanced. I also congratulate my right hon. Friend the Member for Suffolk, Coastal (John Gummer) on giving a clear and moving exposition of the reasons why those of us who believe in the authority of a universal Church find it quite impossible to stay within the Anglican Church if the decision to allow the ordination of women is taken and if this is now to be the nature of the Church. My right hon. Friend's speech was extremely profound, as well as being extremely learned and lucid, and I for one regretted the amount of what I considered to be inappropriate barracking that greeted his extremely serious attempt to try to get away from the secular debate and instead to explain the theological objections that some of us hold most strongly.

Let me deal first with what this issue is not about. It is not about women's rights in the secular sense. I believe that those who would promote the role of women within the Church, of whom I consider myself to be one, have to ask a rather different question from the question on which we have been concentrating. Instead of talking about women fulfilling the sacramental role of the priesthood, to which I shall return, we should ask a much more basic question: has the Church - I use the term in its broadest sense, to mean not just the Anglican Church but the Church universal—got its balance of authority right as between the clerical and the lay? There are many positions of authority held in the Church universal that do not necessarily have to be held by the priesthood. If we consider that rather more fundamental question, the role of women in the Church could be increased. None of us who object to women holding the sacramental priesthood have ever objected to the fact that the Queen is the Supreme Governor of the Church of England, have never objected to women deacons, have never objected to women in the ministry as opposed to the strict definition of the priesthood, and in the Church to which I now belong, I see no reason why there should not be a woman Papal Nuncio. After all, a nuncio is an ambassador and I do not see why a nuncio has necessarily to be a priest.

Let me make it clear from the beginning, I am not opposing the Measure because I do not want to see women fulfilling an important role in the Church. I am opposing it because I believe that it is theologically impossible for women to perform the specific role of the sacramental priesthood. If a woman represents Christ as victim and priest at the Holy Communion, there may just as well be a man who represents the Virgin Mary in a nativity play. Considering the way that the Church of England has been going over the past two or three decades, it would not in the least surprise me if one day I attended a nativity play and found that the Virgin Mary had a beard.

The Church is surrendering its moral authority to purely secular arguments. I am not at all surprised in following today's debate that there is a concentration on the women' rights issues - the House is a secular body, but the Synod is not. The debate in the Synod appalled me because Church matters were being determined with reference to secular approval. As a reason for voting women into the priesthood, the Archbishop of Canterbury, to whom one should be able to look for spiritual, moral and theological leadership, advanced the argument that it would make the Church more acceptable to the secular world.

It seems that the Church of England has not yet learned the basic message that the secular world has been sending back for the past 20 or 30 years: that compromise and a sacrifice of creed to compromise, of doctrine to doubt, and of faith to fashion does not increase congregations or the approval of secular world but decreases congregations, decreases the standing of the Church and undermines its moral authority. Until the Church can send out the straight, simple, uncompromising, courageous and at times unpopular gospel message, all the other compromises that it regularly makes come down merely to rearranging the deckchairs on the Titanic.

I could not share the rosy view of the health of the Church of England to which my right hon. Friend the Member for Selby subscribed in his excellent and able speech. He rightly said that when choosing to be baptised, married or, as he put it, reluctantly to be buried, the majority of the people in the country choose the Church of England through which to conduct those ceremonies. However, the fact remains that during the rest of their lives, there is a minimal number of people in this country who find spiritual sustenance from the Church of England. I will not embarrass my right hon. Friend by drawing comparisons with the ways in which congregations have grown or have been decreasing less in other denominations. One of the reasons for that failure is the way in which the Church looks to the secular world for approval instead of taking its message to the secular world.

I cannot improve on the exposition of my right hon. Friend the Member for Suffolk, Coastal on the issue of authority, but I should like to deal with one point that my right hon. Friend the Member for Selby made. He said that if the Church of Rome could take decisions on the immaculate conception and glorious assumption without reference to the Church of England, the Church of England could take decisions on Orders without reference to the Church of Rome. He entirely ignored the point that my right hon. Friend the Member for Suffolk, Coastal made about the agreement over the last decade between the various members of the - Church universal not to take decisions that will damage the united base of those churches. The decisions to which my right hon. Friend the Member for Selby referred were taken by the Roman Catholic Church many decades ago and they precede this agreement.

He also very cleverly said that it (the decision of the C. of E.) does not make any difference because the magisterium says that Anglican orders are null and void. Therefore it does not make any difference (to Rome) whether those orders will be held by men or women. That is not the point. The difference is the taking of the decision in isolation. I grieve for members of the Church of England who have devoted their lives to the Church but who cannot stay as a result of that single departure from the united Church.

The right hon. Member for Chesterfield (Mr. Benn), in a very amusing but not always relevant speech, said that he hoped the day would come when the Roman Catholic Church would ordain women.

I point out to the right hon. Gentleman and to those who are uttering sedentary approval that it has taken us 400 years to get round to forgiving Galileo and I do not think that the right hon. Member for Chesterfield or I will see a Roman Catholic Church that ordains women.

I now want to deal with the package of compensation for those who have been driven out of the Church by this Measure. If I have derived any amusement from this terrible, grievous and serious subject it is the sight of so many hon. Members who always cry out for employees' rights and for justice and equity brushing aside the inequity and injustice of this provision. The right hon. Member for Chesterfield asked whether Cranmer would have gone if instead of facing the stake he had faced a cheque. Even before this compensation package is in place or any money is available, at least 60 priests have left the Church of England, some of whom are married and have family responsibilities, having sacrificed their rights to that compensation in many cases. There may be no stake for them, but there is no cheque either. I find any condemnation or ridicule of the consciences of those who could not stay utterly offensive and out of keeping with the way in which we should be debating this.

I find the financial provisions Measure entirely inadequate. As my right hon. Friend the Member for Selby said, it does not cover, except in a discretionary sense, a man who has spent five years studying at theological college, a further two years as curate, who has been ordained for 30 years in the Church of England, whose wife has given up her career to support his priesthood but who is, instead of an incumbent of a parish in the Church of England, a serving missionary overseas and is not therefore covered by this compensation. The case I cite is an actual one, not a theoretical one.

There is no coverage, except under discretion, for those who are serving as chaplains - for example, to the armed services or to regional health authorities - although such people might previously have been parish priests. There is no protection for them. Nor will they have protection under ordinary law as a result of the Measure. If they feel that they cannot stay, they will have no protection against constructive dismissal if they are employed by a third party - for example, a regional health authority.

If monks and nuns in religious orders, who have taken vows of poverty and have no resources of their own - and who had reasonably believed that, at the end of their lives they would be cared for by their order - feel, as a result of this Measure, that they cannot stay, they too will have no automatic compensation.

I believe that this Measure is unpassable as it stands. I had originally thought that I would be obliged to vote for the compensation Measure because the worst of all worlds would be that we pass an order in favour of ordaining women but not an order for compensation for those whom this drives out of their livelihood. I am grateful to the hon. Member for Birkenhead (Mr. Field) for making clear that that will not be the result of voting against compensation Measure. The one cannot be valid with the other, even if there is a huge vote in favour of ordination of women.

Those who believe in justice and equity for the people who have no resources of their own, and who will not be covered by this Measure, should know that if the compensation package is rejected, it will not mean that no one will get compensation; it will mean that the legislation will have to be reworked.

I very much regret the inadequate compensation package. We have had a year since the Synod decision last November. Too little was done in advance of that decision the attitude was, "Oh well, we have another five years. The Measure will not be passed." No sense of urgency was shown before that decision to have in place, at the time it was taken, a proper package that people could respect and take into account when voting for the main Measure.

There has been no sense of urgency since then. There has been ill-concealed panic and some hasty patch-ups, but no great sense of urgency to get to the bottom of the compensation provisions and present them to the House in a form which at least meets our standards of justice whatever our doctrinal objections to the main Measure may be. I have listened to the glowing accounts of the Ecclesiastical Committee's work - which was indeed difficult and complicated - but if the early Apostles had shown the same sense of urgency as the Church of England in its approach to moral issues and this compensation package, we would still be worshipping Zeus. The Church of England has failed its own members.

We have heard a lot, particularly from those in favour of the Measure, about the women who have waited patiently within the Church, sat it out and prayed for the resolution that they desired. Those in favour ask why we should be sympathetic to people who have lost the argument when those women have waited patiently for all these years. The answer is that the terms were never changed for the women who waited patiently. When they came into communion with the Church, when they took confirmation, even when they took ordination as deacons, they knew the terms that the Church was setting out. Those who were confirmed and ordained decades ago - like the clergyman to whom I referred, who is now a serving missionary and excluded from compensation - came into the Church on one set of terms and on one doctrine to which they subscribed, which has now been changed over their heads. That is the fundamental difference.

If those who exhibit disagreement with what I am saying were not so wholly taken up with the argument about women's rights —which is not the main argument —would feel strongly about the injustice and inequity of the compensation package.

Let me make a plea to hon. Members. The way, in which they vote on the first Measure must be a matter of conscience, but the second Measure is another issue. The people to whom I have referred look to us to ensure that the position is somewhat better than it is now: only the House can afford them protection.

I am a member of the laity. It is relatively easy—in physical and financial terms, if not in spiritual terms—for members of the laity to leave the Church. But there are many missionaries, monks, nuns and chaplains for whom it will not be at all easy and this Measure denies them any help.

The way in which my right hon. Friend the Member for Selby proposed the motion showed, in large measure, the attitude that I hope the House will adopt. Even if hon. Members cannot understand the reasons involved, I ask them to understand that the matter goes well beyond rights and secular concerns. The sacramental nature of the priesthood is precious, and some people will never be about to come round to the change. At least 60 clergy have already left the Church, and I believe that many more will go when the Measure is passed and the first priestess ordained - because they will then be confronted with the utter reality, and will know that there is no turning back .

Members of the laity can make the decision that the right hon. Member for Chesterfield suggested was so easy .We can just go, albeit with a huge struggle; but the clergy cannot, and they are not well covered by the compensation Measure. The hon. Member for Southwark and Bermondsey and my right hon. Friend the Member for Selby have more or less admitted it. What will determine whether those people receive any protection is the amount of money that the Church Commissioners have—and, we know, the Church Commissioners are facing a black hole of £800 million, which is not entirely accounted for.

I think it important that we do not, at any rate, vote for the second Measure. As for the first, I seek to persuade no one. I think that the issue of the sacramental priesthood very personal: it is based on a person's own spirituality belief, prayer and receipt of the Holy Spirit. I do seek to persuade the House, however, to recognise the grievous position that those in holy orders who share my views—there are some in my own family—now face.

I do not believe that the Church has yet done all that it may. I do not believe that the provisions outlined by my right hon. Friend the Member for Selby, which will sustain the freedom to dissent, are sustainable. They are okay for an immediate transition, but I do not believe that the conscience clause will be worth the paper that it is not written on in 10 years' time in the Church of England.

I think that we shall find a self-selecting Church where

vocations are not recognised for priests who do not believe in the ordination of women, where preferment is denied to bishops, or would-be bishops, who do not believe in the ordination of women. The transition period may be quite satisfactory, but it is unsustainable. The Measure, as drawn, is designed to be unsustainable. It is designed not to be written down as legally binding forever. I think that we have given a raw deal.

The Church had a simple option. It could have included certain specified categories of people and still had an open category for discretion. It could have included those people within the statutory compensation package. It did not. I am not respectful of the way that the Church of England has put its message across in recent years. That is no secret to anybody, but contrary to the views of the right hon. Member for Chesterfield and the hon. Member for Southwark and Bermondsey, who spoke as a member of the Ecclesiastical Committee, although the division between myself and the Church of England is very deep, although the disrespect that I feel for a lot of it—but not all of It—is deep, I never want to see that Church disestablished. If the price that we have to pay for having an established Church is that unbelievers and others will be voting on Anglican Measures, it is a price worth paying, if the other option is finally to remove the tenuous spirituality of this country, where only the recognition of an established Church, through having a crown which holds its authority as a result of a coronation by an Archbishop of Canterbury, gives us religion in schools. If we cut those links, it will be the death of spirituality in Britain. I do not believe that the Church of England has done much to promote it.

1993-1995

The Catholic Times

Between October 1993 and July 1995, Ann Widdecombe wrote a weekly article for the Catholic Times. Below are two of her favourites. The first comments on the uproar following a decision of a Church of England Vicar to ban an adulterer from communion and the second on the controversy which arose when it became known that the new Bishop of Durham had a twenty six year old conviction for indecent behavior.

* * *

Discipline - Dirty Word in the Current Climate

The Catholic Times June 1994

A vicar called Peter Irwin-Clark has upset some of his parishioners who have called him unchristian. His activities have found their way into the national press, where they have been the subject of much comment, particularly the tabloids. What new scandal is this, you may ask, that it causes such commotion?

In fact all the vicar has done is to ban from his church a pair of parishioners who have left their spouses to live with each other.

I can remember a time when the entire parish would have been scandalised had the vicar NOT taken this course of action. It would have been utterly unthinkable that two such persons would have been admitted to communion alongside the abandoned and lawfully wed spouses. Indeed even the secular world had its standards then, but long ago these were replaced by a thing called tolerance which has now been elevated to the status of the supreme virtue.

As the retiring and distinguished headmaster of Eton said recently everything now goes except intolerance.

Yet why should we tolerate what is wrong? Breaking vows solemnly taken before God is wrong. Hurting children by dividing families is wrong. Deserting those who depend upon ones love is wrong. How can a vicar who will not tolerate this sort of wrong be called unchristian?

Of course individuals must not pass judgement on other individuals. We do not know what heartache, what stress or what suffering precede other people's decisions, but there are those who have a duty to pass judgement and who fail in that same duty if they do not.

If this were not the case the legal system would grind to a halt with no judges, juries or magistrates.

Vicars are responsible for the spiritual welfare of their flock and must take whatever action they think appropriate to maintain Christian standards and that includes intolerance of unchristian behaviour. Perhaps if there were a few more Peter Irwin-Clarks about the Church of England would be held in more respect.

A certain amount of intolerance is what is essential if there are to be any standards at all. It is no good saying "Here are the rules, but by all means, feel free to break them. "

Secular law could not function in such a fashion and Christian law should be more exacting than the secular, not less so. It is no wonder the children are so confused. Any concept of setting an example plays a very poor second to what is most convenient.

Children who grew up before the sixties played their havoc with our concepts of social order knew what was regarded as right and wrong. Their parents, teachers and Church spoke with one voice. There was a social consensus as to the standards the young should be taught. That did not necessarily mean they grew up to practise those standards but it did mean that they paused for thought before abandoning them.

Irregular living arrangements were not easily tolerated and therefore there was every incentive not to embark on them. If you did do so you knew why and the motivation was strong enough to overcome the difficulties which the society around you would be sure to put in your path.

That kind of difficult decision is a far cry from today's pattern of drifting into lifestyles and drifting out again, of taking solemn vows and breaking them at the first call of temptation, of signing up to a code of conduct until it no longer suits you and of expecting that no matter what you do it will always be acceptable.

Discipline is a dirty word in the current climate and has been for a distressingly long time; as for self-discipline, the concept is now blatantly regarded as ridiculous.

What, refuse to hurt someone else at the expense of gratifying ones own wishes? What justification should anyone seek but instant wish fulfilment? Objectivity no longer applies and subjectivity is all.

'I shall' has replaced 'Thou shalt not' and now we expect even the Church to bless such a substitution. At any rate some of Rev. Irwin-Clark's parishioners do. That way lies moral anarchy and if the secular world is fool enough to adopt it there is no need for the Christian Church to be so daft. Thank God for the Pope, the catechism, Veritatis Splendor and the Rev. Peter Irwin-Clark.

Michael Turnbull

The Catholic Times

Michael Turnbull, the new Anglican Bishop elect of Durham, who was convicted twenty-six years ago of an act of gross indecency, brings credit on the Church of England. Those who are baying for his resignation do not.

The Bishop does not deny, excuse or attempt to present his crime in a less grave light. He admits it, expresses shame and repentance and is grateful for God's forgiveness. That however is not enough for unforgiving mortals including a number of Durham clergy. Apparently they are far too virtuous to be represented by a mere sinner or to have one placed in authority over them.

It is just as well that this self-righteous bunch were not around in the days of the early church when authority was invested in those guilty of the most appalling sins. A frolic in a public convenience with a consenting adult may be rather distasteful but it does not even begin to measure up to killing off a few saints or to denying all knowledge of our Lord. Whatever would these clergy have made of St. Paul and the first head of our Church? Of course we know what our Lord made of them and He did not wait twenty-six years to put them in positions of the highest trust. Just in case that group of clergy have not yet realised it someone— preferably the Archbishop of Canterbury—should spell out for them the simple fact of Christian life, namely that Christ came to earth for sinners.

Of course those who seek to make a meal out of the Bishop's difficulties accuse him of hypocrisy. It is wrong, they claim, for him not to have been more sympathetic towards homosexual clergy given his own single lapse from grace. Indeed? Presumably then St. Peter should never have condemned a liar given his own three treacherous lies? Why then was he found having Ananias and Sapphira struck down for lying within months—not twenty-six years—of his own offence? Was St. Paul really supposed to take the line that: slaying Christians was quite O.K. really because he had once done it himself?

On this basis St. Philip would never have warned against snobbery nor St. Thomas against doubt nor any of the apostles against vanity or jealousy.

Indeed if it is hypocrisy which we are looking for perhaps we should stick a microphone under the turned up noses of these clergy and see whether they say " ...as we forgive those who trespass against us"? Do they preach redemption at Easter or do they suggest that perhaps Christ was a bit hasty to pardon the dying thief?

Do they not fear judgement themselves or do they suppose that the terrible words "for with what judgement ye judge ye shall be judged and with what measure ye mete it shall be measured to You again" apply to everyone but themselves? Not only do they race to pick up the first stone but they are falling over each other to cast it.

Strange is it not? Wouldn't one have thought that after the last Bishop of Durham a repentant sinner would be a vast improvement?

The Archbishops of Canterbury and York are standing by their choice. Quite right too but I wish they would be a bit sterner with the opposition. Why do they not warn all Christians of the dangers of judging others? Doubtless they would say that they do not want to raise the temperature but I have a feeling that Saints Peter and Paul would have lit a very cauldron rather than put up with the rejection of penitents and of the purpose for which Christ came to earth.

I am praying very hard for Michael Turnbull and for his ministry. I do not believe for one moment that all our priests would behave any better than some of these merciless Anglicans but if a church can in all solemnity allow people to administer its sacraments who deny the resurrection itself yet reject those who do truly and earnestly repent of their sins it must surely beg the question of how much further away from God that church can possibly go.

That is not a question which we should be left asking and that is why it is imperative that Michael Turnbull is enthroned this month and why it is imperative that those Durham clergy who, oppose that enthronement should repent of their sins as publicly as he has done or else forever hold their peace.

As for the newspaper which enlivened the nation's breakfast

tables with the detail of that incident twenty six years ago, perhaps it should now publish a selection of the sins of its own staff in order that we may judge whether it is right that such people should bring us the news of others' wrongdoing. Oops,I forgot. Tabloid journalists, like some Anglican clergy, are quite without sin. They must be to judge from the hail of stones which emanates from their pages.

Home Affairs: 'Something of the Night'

In May 1997 Ann Widdecombe made one of the most controversial speeches heard in recent years in the House of Commons. Speaking during the contest for the leadership of the Conservative Party, she spoke out against her previous boss at the Home Office and fellow Kent MP, Michael Howard. Howard was also a contender for the Party leadership. Ann Widdecombe had served under Howard at the Home Office as Prisons Minister but had had a serious disagreement with him over his summary dismissal of the Director General of the Prisons Service, Derke Lewis. Lewis had by this time published a book outlining the circumstances of his departure. Ann Widdecombe greatly regretted not resigning at the time over the issue and felt that she now had no alternative but to outline her concerns to the House. She did this in the full knowledge that anything she said would damage, probably fatally, Michael Howard's leadership challenge. This speech came to be known as the "Something of the Night" speech, despite the fact that the words did not figure in the text at all. Despite her fear that the speech could turn her colleagues against her, it turned out to be the making of her.

* * *

Madam Speaker, I am very grateful for the opportunity to speak in this debate, and for your advice that it will be in order for me to concentrate on events that occurred in the Home Office under the last Administration. If my remarks need a current context, they are made in the light of the necessity for the current Home Office Ministers to sort out their proper relationship with the Prison Service and other agencies.

Before embarking on my remarks, I should like to join in the tributes paid to Sir Michael Shersby, and in the congratulations to the Secretary of State for the Home Department, the right hon. Member for Blackburn (Mr. Straw) and the rest of his Front-Bench team. That is probably the nicest thing that I shall say to them for the rest of this Parliament.

I should say two things at the outset because it is now generally known that what I have to say will be less than encouraging to my right hon. and learned Friend the Member for Folkestone and Hythe (Mr. Howard). First, I pay very great and very genuine tribute to his work at the Home Office. He put the protection of the public at the top of the agenda, and he kept it there. His term of office saw a fall in crime and a vast improvement in Her Majesty's prisons. He introduced a raft of measures to make Britain a more orderly place, and had the courage to make much-needed reforms to our widely abused asylum system.

It is therefore with genuine sadness and considerable reluctance, which I have had to overcome, that I turn to the rest of my remarks. But for my utter conviction of their rightness and of the imperative that lies behind them, I should not be making these remarks at all.

Secondly, although my remarks are informed by a number of documents and oral evidence, I shall not identify any individual document or any civil servants and Ministers whom I may quote. If ex-Ministers were to do that, government would become unworkable. However, if my right hon. and learned Friend hears me allude to things that he does not recognise, I will be happy afterwards to point out to him where the words occur.

It is urgently necessary for the House to restore its reputation with the nation. Many of our great institutions are falling into disrepute. I was wretchedly aware of how many people to whom I talked during the Election uttered the sentiment that politicians of all parties are sleazy and corrupt, and principally concerned with their own interests and survival. That is an unjust and distorted picture, and does great disservice to the overwhelming majority of dedicated, honourable and hard-working Members of the House. It is regrettable that the House has been back only five minutes and already there is a corruption story—this time on the Labour Benches—all over our newspapers.

It should alarm us all that the House is now so comprehensively viewed as devoid of honour and a sense of service. In case there are smug looks on the faces of Labour members, I have to say that the Labour party is ill placed to talk of principle when it changed its mind on policy three times in a day merely to win an election. Whatever fun the public make of us, and no matter how upset the public may be by our decisions, it is still essential for there to be an underlying view that Members of the House are just, honourable and truthful. The higher the office the greater that imperative.

Honourable treatment means that we treat those in our power justly and that we do not reject from them defences that we regularly mount for ourselves. I profoundly regret that, in the previous Parliament Ministers were criticised in independent reports and did not resign. I am not saying that they necessarily should have done, but if it is justice for them not to resign, it is also justice for our loyal servants not to resign.

If a party can go to the country and urge that its occasional disasters, however monumental, be overlooked on the basis of its otherwise truly magnificent achievements, it cannot, in honour, deny that same defence to individuals. Regularly to protect and excuse ourselves while visiting serious vengeance on others corrupts justice and demeans office.

Earlier, I alluded to the fact that there had been a great improvement in Her Majesty's prisons under the former Home Secretary. That improvement was the result of the efforts of two men: my right hon. and learned Friend and the former head of the Prison Service, Mr. Derek Lewis.

Mr. Lewis was an outstanding director general. He inherited an appalling and troubled service, which in 14 years we had not got right. Escapes took place daily, assaults were rife, industrial relations were chaotic and financial management poor. Under his vigorous leadership, escapes fell by a staggering 77 per cent. Overcrowding was reduced, despite a sharp rise in the number of prisoners; purposeful activity was increased by hundreds of thousands of hours, despite a reduction in costs per place; industrial relations were transformed; and the private finance initiative was so successfully run that it became a model for the rest of Whitehall.

The agency essentially met all targets set by Ministers and new initiatives, such as reform to home leaves, drug testing and the incentives and earned privileges regimes were successfully implemented. All that was managed within two and a half years.

There was still a great deal to be done - that is common ground - but it would have been unreasonable to expect everything to be achieved in the first 18 months, which is when the escape from Whitemoor occurred. After all although I hesitate to point it out - we still had things to achieve after 18 years.

If people want a snapshot comparison of the Prison Service before Mr. Lewis came and when he left, they need only read the speech of the former Home Secretary my right hon. and learned Friend the Member for Rushcliffe (Mr. Clarke). He referred to the poor state of the Prison Service and correctly and courageously said that Ministers of all parties must take the blame. That speech, which was made in 1992 before the establishment of the agency, should be compared with the speech of my right hon. and learned Friend the Member for Folkestone and Hythe to the Prison Service conference in 1996 - only a few months after Mr. Lewis left - in which he praised to the skies the achievements of the service in the previous three years.

It was for those reasons that Ministers, very senior civil

Servants, the Prisons Board and its non-executives urgently advised the then Home Secretary that he should not dismiss Mr. Lewis. It was for those reasons that two of the four non-executives resigned in protest, and that others chose other forms of making their views known. It was for those reasons that I nearly resigned, and now regret not doing so. I put that on the record: I now regret not doing so. If Mr. Lewis had been an indifferent director general, there would have been less achievement and certainly less support.

The Learmont report—which was used by the Home Secretary to dismiss Mr. Lewis—took no account of that progress; nor did it attempt to measure it, because that was not the general's brief. But, when—two months after Derek Lewis had left—the general was briefed to measure progress on implementation, this time on the Woodcock recommendations, he found: "In the space of less than a year the Prison Service has made more headway than could reasonably have been expected".

Another report produced at that time found that Mr. Lewis had provided visible leadership, and reached other conclusions not compatible with the main Learmont report. One wonders what my right hon. and learned Friend would have made of it if he had had all three reports when reaching his conclusions. It is also worth recording that a previous report on the Whitemoor breakout had specifically exonerated Mr. Lewis of any negligence.

Before I end this section of my remarks, it is worth pointing out that there were serious flaws in the Learmont report in terms of approach and substantiation. I find its credibility severely dented by the fact that, when the General appeared before the Select Committee, it became obvious that he had no idea how escapes were measured and he admitted to simply missing a basic analysis of escape by categorisation of prisoner. Having made a large number of recommendations about Prison Service headquarters, he said that he had not visited the headquarters. The reason he gave was that he did not think that his team would be very welcome.

In a major report on security and organisation, that does not inspire me with confidence. My right hon. and learned Friend is very skilled forensically, and I cannot believe that he was taken in by the superficiality of some of the report. It is hard to conclude other than that the report was his pretext rather than his reason. There is evidence within the Home Office that he had wanted for a long time before that report was produced to remove Mr. Lewis from his post.

In his Spectator article, the former Home Secretary says that any chief executive of a private company who had received such a damning report would have been expected to resign. I say that any chief executive who had secured a 70 per cent improvement in performance would in fact have received the highest rewards.

What did we actually achieve by the dismissal of Mr. Lewis? We had to pay him £220,000 in compensation, in return for which the taxpayer received nothing at all. We had to pay his costs, in the sum of £41,000, in return for which the taxpayer received nothing at all. We had to pay our own costs, in the sum of some £16,000. A most unnecessary bill of more than a quarter of a million pounds was the cost to the general public of my right hon. and learned Friend's decision.

We severely damaged relations with the private sector as we found out when we considered the possibility of running an open competition for Mr. Lewis's job - a possibility from which we quickly retreated. We created a false distinction between policy and operations which has reverberated around the whole of Whitehall not just the Home Office. We have endured swingeing headlines in the press, not least when the Home Office was ignominiously forced to consent to the judgement on the very day that the Conservative faithful were being rallied at the Central Council.

We left the Prison Service without a confirmed leader for five months, and we shattered its morale, just when things had been going well for 10 months. Manpower and time have been taken up by endless briefings and Select Committees—not just the Home Affairs Committee but the Public Service Committee—and the effects of the whole affair still rumble on.

And, for all that, did we eliminate disasters from the Prison Service? No. Only a few months later approximately 541 prisoners were released before the end of their sentences. They did not even have to break out! The fact is that there were disasters in the service before Lewis—including high-profile escapes-disasters in the service during Lewis, and disasters in the service after Lewis; but, as the current director general - to whom I pay considerable tribute - has told the Home Affairs Select Committee, the real progress has been made since the granting of agency status and that was due largely to the man who ran the agency at the time.

Quite apart from the merits of the case, the handling was deplorable—and, personally witnessed by me, was the cause of the distress that has now become public knowledge. The former director general was refused point blank on two occasions the opportunity to discuss the basis on which he was being dismissed. He had filed a large and detailed defence to the Learmont report, which was subsequently published, and even the former Home Secretary acknowledged that defence to be "persuasive and impressive".

My right hon. and learned Friend decided, however, that it painted a different picture of the Prison Service from Learmont's, and that he preferred Learmont's. Mr. Lewis immediately said that the two pictures were compatible, but the Home Secretary would hear no argument on the point. I consider that an amazing act on the part of the head of a Justice Department.

A dismissal meeting on the 15th October lasted 20 minutes; a meeting on the 16th lasted 12 minutes, with, again, the former Home Secretary refusing to hear Mr. Lewis's defence. Although we had had the report on 27 September, a decision was not communicated to Mr. Lewis until 15 October, and he was then given six hours in which to resign. That was subsequently extended, and, in the meantime - although he had been asked to resign and to give notice and was therefore presumably still head of the service - he was not admitted to meetings, and not copied into documents then being prepared for the statement. It is not surprising that Mr. Lewis did not go quietly.

I might add that it was the minutes of those meetings, that convinced me that minutes of meetings may be perfectly accurate without reflecting the tone and full content of the meetings. For example, there was a question of security audit which showed that the then Home Secretary believed that Mr. Lewis had set up security audits only after Whitemoor. In fact, they had been set up before Whitemoor, which suggests that Mr. Lewis did not need a disaster to see the importance of security. That exchange is not recorded.

It has often been said that Mr. Lewis was dismissed because after Whitemoor, he failed to take action to prevent Parkhurst. One could be forgiven for believing that absolutely nothing was going on between the two events. In fact, the opposite is true.

Mr. Lewis had already put in hand additional cameras, alterations to fence height, infra-red screens, alarm-activated static cameras, installation of closed-visit facilities, new methods of recording intelligence, an increase in rub-down searches, routine searching of all staff and visitors, upgraded supervision of visits, the introduction of specialist arms and explosives search teams, local staff training, high-technology searching equipment, the introduction of personal alarms and volumetric control. How can it be claimed he did nothing in that couple of months?!

We all know that, when Ministers come before the House, they sometimes give us coded messages. [Laughter.] These Ministers will do it, too. We know that, if a Minister appears before the House and says, "I have received an important report, and I will publish it shortly," we may truly expect to find it in the Library shortly. If he says, "I will publish it as soon as possible," we know that it will take quite a long time. If he says, "I will publish it in due course," it is going to take a very long time indeed. But if he says, "This report has very serious implications which need very careful examination, and I will not be able to report to the House until that has happened," that means, "By gum! I am leaving this one for my successor."

My right hon. and learned Friend has a most exquisite way with words. On 16 October 1995, when presenting the Learmont report to Parliament, he told the House - hon. Members will find this in column 32 of Hansard - "One particular aspect that I asked Sir John to consider was the extent to which visits should be closed. He recommends that there should be closed visits for exceptional risk category prisoners other than in exceptional circumstances."

He told us: "That coincides with the policy that I introduced in June this year." - (Official Report, 16 October 1995; Vol.264, c.32.).

The use of the word "coincides" is intriguing. It is not unsustainable, but it is a bit curious, because no coincidence whatever was involved.

The Salmon version of the Learmont report specifically recommended that there should not be closed visits, even in Special Security Units. However, my right hon. and learned Friend subsequently wrote to General Learmont and stated in a very brief letter that he had decided that, when the SSU was opened at Whitemoor, closed visits would be implemented, whereupon the obliging general wrote back in five lines thanking him for that input, and stating that it would be reflected in his report.

The final version of the Learmont report totally reversed the original conclusion, and recommended closed visits. That says a great deal about the methodology of the Learmont report, on which I have already commented but it also causes me to raise my eyebrows a little at the choice of words that were used to the House.

When there was a decidedly embarrassing court settlement, a document was put in the Conservative Whips office for the use of Members. That suggests that Members could have used the information to deploy in the House. I think that, had they done so, they would have left themselves open to serious embarrassment.

That document was certainly not written personally by my right hon. and learned Friend: it was produced by Conservative Central Office. But it is inconceivable that it would have arrived in the Whips office if he had thought it inaccurate. That document told Members that the settlement is not an admission that Mr. Lewis was either wrongfully or unfairly dismissed. That statement is sustainable only on the utmost technicality.

I shall read to the House, because they have already been published, as has the foregoing Learmont exchange, by Mr. Lewis in his evidence to the Select Committee and are therefore in the public domain, the exact terms of the Home Office lawyer's letter, our having been told that we admit no wrongful dismissal. The letter states: "For the avoidance of any possible remaining doubt I confirm that notwithstanding the Home Office is unable to admit terminating Mr. Lewis's contract in breach of contract due to the constitutional position of the Crown, it is accepted that, but for that position, your client's employment was terminated otherwise than in accordance with the terms of his contract. Accordingly, my client is willing to compensate Mr. Lewis upon the basis of damages for wrongful dismissal."

No wonder Mr. Lewis described our defence as "a fig leaf so small as to be grossly indecent."

I shall now turn to the censure debate in October 1995. My right hon. and learned Friend said: "On Tuesday the Leader of the Opposition made three allegations:".

He went on to list them and said that the first one was "that I personally told Mr. Lewis that the governor of Parkhurst Should be suspended immediately;"

He listed the other allegations, and said: "Each and every one of the allegations is untrue" (Official Report, 19 October' 1995; Vol. 264, c. 524.)

In other words. he categorically denied in the House that he had personally told Mr. Lewis that the Governor of Parkhurst should be suspended immediately.

Some hon. Members may have watched "Newsnight" On

Tuesday 13 May, in which my right hon. and learned Friend was far less categoric. He said of Mr. Lewis: "I gave him the benefit of my opinion in strong language."

I can tell the House that the "Newsnight" version is the correct one.

There is ample documentary evidence that my right hon. and learned Friend did indeed personally tell Mr. Lewis that the Governor of Parkhurst should be suspended. The atmosphere at that meeting, attested to by the documents is of fury and confrontation. I was told in a personal note by one of those present: "This was the subject of the worst disagreement. The Home Secretary wanted suspension, Derek Lewis adamantly refused."

Another document recorded: "the discussion generated a lot more heat than light... and you made it clear that your preference was for suspension."

The warning that Derek Lewis has said that he received after he had been asked to reconsider his decision—that "this is all getting white hot and I do not want it to become nuclear"—is documented within the Department.

I say categorically to the House that the documents in the Department and the recollections of the civil servants and Ministers concerned show that Derek Lewis was told that the Governor of Parkhurst should be suspended, and that he was told to take time to reconsider his decision when he refused. That is a very different picture from the one that was painted in the House on 19 October 1995, when all that my right hon. and learned Friend would admit to was wondering whether suspension might be more appropriate, and asking questions. I can only ask the House to imagine what "white hot wondering" or "questions going nuclear" or "querying in strong language" consist of.

To tell Mr. Lewis that the Governor of Parkhurst should be suspended is completely different from instructing Mr. Lewis. My right hon. and learned Friend has frequently said that he did not instruct Mr. Lewis - and he did not: there is common ground on that. However, he told him that the governor of Parkhurst should be suspended. The threat of instruction was distinct and was the second allegation, and we need to make sure that the two are disentangled.

The reason why the right hon. Member for Blackburn, now the Secretary of State for the Home Department, came to such grief in the debate on 19 October 1995 was that there was insufficient precision in using terms, and my right hon. and learned Friend is very precise in his terms. In the debate, my right hon. and learned Friend was asked by the hon. Member for Sunderland, South (Mr. Mullin): "Mr. Lewis says that he was given a deadline by the right hon. and learned Gentleman by which to agree to the removal of Mr. Marriott, after which he would be overruled. Is that true?"

My right hon. and learned Friend replied categorically: "There was no question of overruling the director general".(Official Report, 19 October 1995; Vol.264, c. 520.)

Oh, yes, there was. As he rather belatedly admitted last week, and as documentary evidence within the Department shows, after Mr. Lewis had been asked to reconsider his decision, my right hon. and learned Friend took advice on whether he could instruct Derek Lewis to suspend Mr. Marriott - this bearing in mind that he had told the House that he had not personally told Mr. Lewis that Marriott should be suspended.

But my right hon. and learned Friend was now carrying matters to the extent of seeking to instruct Mr. Lewis, and, after consultation with the Cabinet Office and legal advisers in the Department, he was advised that he could not instruct him. Therefore, it cannot be said that there was no question of overruling the director general. The question was asked, it was pursued, and it was answered in the negative.

In the October 1995 debate, my right hon. and learned Friend was asked whether Mr. Lewis had left the meeting to consider the deadline that the Secretary of State had set him to reconsider his decision. The former Home Secretary replied: "I have no idea, at this distance in time, why he left the meeting". (Official Report, 19 October 1995; Vol.264, c.521.).

However, the day before, he had received an account of that meeting, which clearly showed that Mr. Lewis was asked when he left the meeting to "talk further" and " think it through". I cannot believe that my right hon. and learned Friend's formidable memory should cause him to feel that 24 hours is a great distance in time.

In column 523 of the Official Report, my right hon. and learned Friend referred to minutes of the disputed meeting which he had placed in the Library. He told the House that the minutes were the detailed official account, and that he was doing his best to give the House a full account. But those minutes are not a full account. For example they omit the very important fact that Mr. Lewis was invited to reconsider his decision. They are not the most detailed account. That would be the transcription of the private secretary's notebooks. The minutes are silent on matters that are well documented elsewhere.

There has also been some uncertainty about why the former Governor of Parkhurst was moved from his post on the day that my right hon. and learned Friend made his statement, rather than within a few days, as the director general and operational director had intended. I have now seen detailed evidence that makes it clear the it was only a transcript of the words used by my right hon. and learned Friend to the House, which was transmitted to Parkhurst, which caused that change.

Hon. Members will note that there has been much interest in the press this week as to whether there was a direct threat from the former Home Secretary to the former director general that my right hon. and learned Friend would have to consider overruling him if, when he had reconsidered his decision, he did not come to a different view. We know that he was sent out to reconsider his decision. We know that, during that time advice was taken on whether he could indeed be overruled. It is very strange that my right hon. and learned Friend refused to answer that question 14 times on "Newsnight" last week, and was so uncharacteristically tongue-tied that he could not explain, as he later claimed that he was simply unsure about that element of such traumatic disagreement, and needed to check the papers

Although it was not debated in the House on 19 October, questions had been raised in that week as to whether the Home Secretary had threatened not only to overrule Mr. Lewis, but to sack him. This was 10 months before he was sacked. I can confirm that he did talk about sacking him that day, but not to Mr. Lewis himself. Mr. Lewis subsequently found out from a third party, but it shows the degree of ferocity that existed in that fateful meeting.

Therefore, the questions to my fight hon. and learned Friend are these. Why did he say that he had not personally told Mr. Lewis that Mr. Marriott should be suspended immediately, when he had? Why did he say that there was no question of overruling Mr. Lewis, when the question had been pursued as far as consulting the Cabinet Office and legal advisers? Why did he say that he could not recall at that distance in time why Mr. Lewis had been asked to leave the meeting, when he had received only the previous day an account of that meeting which showed that Mr. Lewis had been asked to reconsider his decision?

Why did my right hon. and learned Friend say that he was giving the House a full account, when he well knows that important issues that were discussed in the House were in fact omitted from the minutes that he laid before it as a full account? Will he now, to clear any doubt at all that may exist in the minds of hon. Members, ask the current Home Secretary to release the full transcript of the meeting, minus of course anything that might have involved security in our prisons?

I should say that, intriguingly, when I asked the Home Office whether I could have access to the document, I was denied, on the perfectly proper basis that I had not been involved in the meeting at the time. I then said, "Ah, but the document does then exist," and I was told, "Yes, but it might need some adjustment."

My right hon. and learned Friend has a problem, in that his first reaction to attack is denial and refuge in semantic prestidigitation. Why did he not simply come to the House on 19 October and say, "So what? Yes, I did tell the director general that Marriott should have been suspended. Yes, I did feel about it so strongly that I put huge pressure on him. Yes, I did tell him to reconsider his decision, and, yes, I did consider overruling him? It was just too important not to consider it." Why on earth did he not say that, to what I have no doubt would have been high cheers from the then Government Benches? He could not do so because he had dug a hole for himself over policy and operations, and he would never have had to dig such a hole had he been prepared to keep the director general in place.

The issues before the House are not whether Marriott should have been suspended; I think that he should have been. They are not whether there was a smoking fax; the Opposition were confused. They are not about the precise form of words used in evidence to the Select Committee on the Marriott removal. It is purely the matter of statements made in the House on 19 October to which I am addressing myself. As a matter of fact, as I have said, I do believe that the former Home Secretary would have been right had he taken all those actions. It was simply that he told the House that they were not taken.

In the winding-up speech on 19 October 1995, I said that there was no doubt of the validity of the statements made to the Select Committee by the then Home Secretary and the then director general of the Prison Service, but, even as I stood at that Dispatch Box and spoke those words, I was starting to have very severe doubts about some of the statements that had been made in the House on that day. Even so, for a long time, I could not be sure that actual words, as opposed to tone and impression, could be challenged. All manner of things made me determined to carry out the analysis that I have now carried out; and I regret that among those things was the treatment of Mr. Lewis after he left the Prison Service.

My right hon. and learned Friend has been defending himself

this week against various statements that have come out—they have come from me, most of them. None of those defences has taken us much further forward. Asked why he refused 14 times on "Newsnight" to deny something that he had already categorically denied in the House, he said that he would have to check the record, but that seems, in the words of an article in The Economist "a strange lapse for a high powered lawyer who had been challenged many times before on this precise point."

He then offered a defence in The Spectator, saying, significantly, that civil servants would have checked his account and they would have told him if it he been wrong.

I have two comments to make on that statement. The first is that it contains the familiar sound of looking for scapegoats. Can my right hon. and learned Friend really not take responsibility for what he said himself? Secondly it begs the question: supposing the civil servants had pointed out an inaccuracy, would he have rushed down to the House to correct it? He did not do so when he inadvertently—I stress that it was inadvertent-misled the House of Commons Select Committee over geophones.

In January 1995, my right hon. and learned Friend told the Select Committee on Home Affairs that money had not been switched from construction projects, including geophones, to building new house blocks. Indeed, he made the clear and unambiguous statement that additional money had been provided for the house blocks. Many months later, he was advised by his civil servants that this was wrong and he was also advised that statements that he had made in the House in connection with the timing of the decision to install geophones were also wrong. The issue was important, because the absence of geophones had been criticised by Sir John Learmont.

When I pointed out that no correction had been made the former Home Secretary issued another of his statements. He said that he had sought immediate advice from Derek Lewis, who had advised that there was no practical significance to his answer, as funds were found for the geophones from other sources.

Therefore, he advised the former Home Secretary that probably he had not misled the Committee, and the former Home Secretary takes refuge in that advice from Derek Lewis. It must be one of the few times that he was grateful for advice from Derek Lewis.

My right hon. and learned Friend omits to point out that, in two succeeding memoranda, his own Prison Service monitoring unit stuck to its guns and said that the statements were misleading; that they did not consist of the full account, which Ministers are obliged to give under "Questions of Procedure for Ministers"; and that, had officials given such information, they would have been obliged to correct it.

But no correction was ever made, despite the fact that an ideal opportunity was presented when the Learmont report was published. A very bland, all-encompassing statement could then have been made, to the effect that the detailed analysis replaced all previous information and corrected any previous information inadvertently wrongly given.

My right hon. and learned Friend has made much of how he is the one to take tough decisions. Tough decisions concern a great deal more than instant law and instant dismissals. The toughest decision of all that he would have had to take was to come to the House on 16 October, told it that a damning report had been received, but that half its recommendations had already been implemented or were actively being put in hand; that the progress of the Prison Service under the director general was of such outstanding quality that he was continuing with my right hon. and learned Friend's personal support; and that he, the Home Secretary also had no intention of resigning, because there was no direct connection between himself and what had happened.

That would have been tough, because the then Opposition would have howled for a head, and, if they were not given Mr. Lewis's, they might have howled for that of my right hon. and learned Friend, but we had a majority, so there was no reason to suppose that they would get it. However, he had been through that terrible sort of confrontation in the House in January, immediately after the Parkhurst breakout, and he was not quite tough enough to face it again in October.

Courage and toughness are both more than instant law and instant dismissal. We demean our high office if we mistreat our public servants. As hon. Members, we demean ourselves if we come to the House to indulge in a play of words and make statements which, although they may not be untrue - they never are in the House - may be unsustainable.

My decision to do what I have done today was extremely difficult to reach, and I have agonised over it for months. One of the worst moments was when I decided that I would do it. I knew how shocked, hurt and upset not only my right hon. and learned Friend but many of my colleagues would be, but I formed the view that I could do no other. I reached my decision in the interests of giving very belated justice to Mr. Lewis, of giving some comfort to his wife Louise - who supported him faithfully while he gave us seven days a week looking after the Prison Service - partly of clearing my own conscience, although that is my problem, because I should have resigned at the time and did not - [HON. MEMBERS: "Hear, hear."] Yes, I agree.

I reached that view also to draw to the attention of the House the overwhelming necessity for the Leader of the Opposition— whoever he will be—and the new Prime Minister to clean up Parliament's image in the eyes of the British people. It is not enough to preserve our own positions at all costs. When we occupy high positions, and certainly when we occupy such positions in Justice Departments, justice must be our first concern.

I am aware that I probably will not be forgiven for my decision by some Conservative Members until the day I leave Parliament. If I had not done what I have done today, however, I would not have forgiven myself until I left Parliament and beyond.

Fox Hunting

In November 1997 Ann Widdecombe was once more on the backbenches, following her attack on Michael Howard. Revelling in this first taste of freedom after six and a half years as a Minister she spoke in the second reading debate of a Private Member's Bill to abolish hunting. The speech was generally acclaimed as the best in the debate and has been much quoted since. It also drew the rare accolade of applause in the House of Commons.

* * *

I congratulate the hon. Member for Worcester (Mr. Foster) on his choice of subject. I particularly congratulate him on his courage in introducing a controversial Bill so early in his time in the House.

I also congratulate the hon. Member for Wansdyke (Dan Norris) on his maiden speech and on having the courage to make it in such a debate. His predecessor Jack Aspinwall—was much respected on both sides of the House. I am grateful for the tribute paid to him.

Having started on that friendly note, I should like to engage in one of my favourite sports - trying to flush out the Prime Minister. The hon. Member for Worcester told the House that the Prime

Minister supported the Bill. I am pleased to hear that. Does that support extend to making parliamentary time available? I hope that I shall be assisted in the resolution of that query by the spokesman for the Government. I hope that he will help me to flush out the Prime Minister.

On 15 April—hon. Members may recall that was in the middle of the general election campaign—the current Prime Minister, in his then role of Leader of the Opposition wrote to Tony Banks M.P. He said: "Our policy is to have a free vote in Parliament on whether hunting with hounds should be banned by legislation. If such a vote is passed, it will be a decision made by Parliament and parliamentary time will be made available for appropriate legislation to progress in the normal way."

I repeat: "Parliamentary time will be made available".

If the House votes in favour of the Bill, I hope that the Prime Minister will honour his promise and will make time available, not for a measure on licensing or some other watered-down proposition, but for the measures in the Bill. We have heard a lot of talk about what the House of Lords will do. I want to know what the Prime Minister will do .

I turn now to some of the arguments made in the debate. Yes, the fox is exceptionally cruel. When it goes into a hen-house it is concerned not only with getting a good supper but with having a horrible time with the hens. Does that mean that we should take our standards from the fox?

Is it proposed that, because a fox eats a couple of guinea pigs in a nasty way, the House should take its standards from the fox? I find that proposition amazing, as I have some of the other arguments advanced today.

It is argued that if we abolish hunting, we will abolish jobs. If we abolish crime, we will put all the police out of work. If we abolish ill health, we will put all the nurses and doctors out of work. Does anyone seriously suggest that we must preserve at all costs crime and ill health because they keep people in jobs?

The Bill proposes penalties and its opponents have today

protested that there must be consensus before we lock people up, that if there is a large body of opinion that says that something is okay, we must not lock up the practitioners. What about the legalisation of cannabis? A sizeable body of opinion, with which I am totally at odds, says that cannabis is all right. I defend to the hilt society's right to lock up the purveyors of cannabis. I defend also to the hilt - although this will not be so acceptable to Labour Members - our right to lock up people who did not pay their poll tax when it was a lawfully levied tax.

If this democratically elected House decides that hunting is against the law, it is our right to exact penalties against those who wilfully break the law. We will be penalising not the fact that they like to hunt but the fact that they break the law. I do not believe that the sort of people who tell me that they want to carry on hunting are the sort who would wilfully break the law. There seems to be an underlying assumption that, if this Bill is passed, such people will go out breaking the law. Frankly, I doubt it. If Parliament changes the law, I believe that people will largely obey it and that we are entitled to take action against those who do not.

It is important to ask ourselves a simple question. Is hunting so wrong that we wish to abolish it? If it is, all else flows from that. We do not need to be concerned about jobs or liberties to do wrong; we need only ask whether it is so wrong that it should be abolished.

My problem with hunting is not that I contest the right of farmers to practise pesticide. Hunting is a most ineffective pesticide. Its supporters have tried to have it both ways by saying that they do not kill too many foxes but also that they kill so many that it is a good pesticide. In fact, nine tenths of fox control is done by shooting, not hunting.

Hunting is not a pesticide, so we must ask what it is. It is cruelty. I am not against killing foxes or culling deer. I am against the chase, the cruelty involved, in prolonging terror of a living, sentient being that is running for its life. We are asked to believe these beings are laughing.

When the deer is running, can feel the hounds closing in and knows that its strength is not going to last, it is uproariously funny. If it is so funny, why do not those who favour hunting take a trip to Kenya and stand unprotected in a lion reserve and see if they enjoy the hunt? I admit that I might enjoy watching it. Prolongation of terror is wrong. Those who practise it when there are alternatives that are already widely practised do wrong. Yes, the scenes of a hunt are splendid, so splendid that they are all over my dining room curtains, but they are colourful scenes of olde England, and in olde England, not in modern Britain, they belong.

Standards and Privileges

In November 1997 Ann Widdecombe resigned from the powerful Standards and Privileges Committee in protest against its treatment of Neil Hamilton in particular and its procedures in general. While holding no view as to Hamilton's guilt or innocence, she defended his right to cross examine witnesses and to have access to an appeal,neither of which had been granted to him. The speech threw into question the self regulation of Parliament.

* * *

I want to take this opportunity to bring to the House my concerns about the way in which self-regulation is operating - or, as I would contend, failing to operate - in this important area. It is an important area because if we cannot regulate ourselves in a way that commands confidence, both in this House and among the public at large, we certainly cannot aspire to regulate others.

I believe that the report into the investigation of Neil Hamilton was a travesty - a travesty of natural justice, and the result of a deplorable shambles. It is urgent that we put together proper procedures in this House so we never have that sort of a shambles again. There is general agreement among Members of all parties that the current procedures are inadequate.

First, let me say that I do not criticise the thoroughness with which Sir Gordon Downey carried out his investigation; it would be quite wrong to do so. The report involved the detailed amassing of highly complex evidence, and reports that there was a falling out between Sir Gordon Downey and the Committee are very much exaggerated. I pay tribute to the report that he produced. Nor am I necessarily convinced that Mr. Hamilton was innocent of the main charge - taking cash for questions in brown envelopes from Mohammed Al Fayed. My disquiet over the report has nothing to do with any view that Mr. Hamilton might be innocent. It is straightforwardly that I do not believe I can make a judgment as to whether he was innocent or guilty on the basis of the procedures that were adopted.

It is disturbing that this House, which should set an example of justice and fair dealing, was presented with a report against which Mr. Hamilton had no appeal. My concern would apply to anybody else in such a situation; this is not special pleading for Mr. Hamilton . It is a basic tenet of British justice that there can be an appeal against a guilty verdict. We assume the verdict was guilty because it was indicative of the shambles which occurred that no two members of the Committee were able to agree on what the report was telling the House.

The Chairman said that Sir Gordon's findings stood, which meant that the verdict was guilty; but the hon. Member for Ross, Skye and Inverness, West (Mr. Kennedy) told the House that there was no clear verdict, so it was not proven, which was also my understanding of our conclusion. That is why we removed one set of words, saying that we endorsed the findings, and substituted another, saying that we could find no practical way of adding to or subtracting from them. The House was entitled to a clear statement of what we had found, rather than several confused versions from different members of the Committee.

Throughout our proceedings we were bedevilled by the fact that there were no clear, agreed procedures. I never before sat on a

Committee in which we made up our procedures as we went along, but that is exactly what happened. We could not agree on what our remit was or what our procedures should be. We ended by reducing justice to the decision of a single inquisitor, against which there was no effective appeal.

It was farcical that, when Mr. Hamilton appeared before us and talked at us—I cannot think of any other way of expressing it—for nearly two and a half hours, we were not allowed to ask any questions. If we thought that he had contradicted himself or that something was unclear, we could not ask about it; we had to sit there in silence and absorb the onslaught—that is what it was—for two and a half hours. That is profoundly unsatisfactory. At the end, I was none the wiser. I had heard a great deal that had raised an awful lot of questions in my mind, but because I could not ask questions I was neither wiser nor better informed.

We could not examine the main witnesses against Mr. Hamilton. Mr. Al Fayed was not called before the Committee, and we could not examine those who said that they had been involved in the dispatch of the money, so we had no basis on which to assess a report that had been challenged. That was our real problem, because there were no serious challenges to the facts in all the other reports before us; there were pleas in mitigation, writings to the Committee to apologise and drawings of our attention to other matters, but there was no real challenge to facts. On the occasion when there was an extremely serious challenge to facts we did not have the procedures to deal with it.

We examined Sir Gordon Downey's huge and extremely thorough report and we knew that it would take a very long time, involve a great deal of complexity, and demand resources that we possibly did not have, to re-examine the questions from scratch. The answer to that was not to shrug our shoulders and have done with it, but to come back to the House and say that we were stuck and needed a clear remit and guidance on how we should proceed.

We have to decide whether the Select Committee on

Standards and Privileges is an appellate body. Should it hear appeals against the Commissioner's findings? If not, who is to hear such appeals? Or are we seriously suggesting that we should create in the House a situation, unique in this country, in which a finding can blight someone's career prospects, and even preclude membership of the House, but no appeal is possible? Surely that must be unacceptable.

We have to decide what appeal there should be. Should it be heard by the Committee or by some other body? Should practising lawyers be involved? What should we do? Is the Committee simply a sentencing and administrative body, or is it an investigative body that determines guilt and innocence? Those questions, incredibly, have not been sorted out. We carried out investigations if that is the right word - into the conduct of Members of Parliament, without an answer to the basic question: what is the purpose of the Committee?

The purpose of the Committee determines very much what its composition should be. I regret the fact that it has been downgraded in composition. A Select Committee on Standards and Privileges, sitting in judgment on Members of Parliament, and occasionally quite senior ones, should itself be a senior Committee. I regret the fact that the Leader of the House does not chair it. The Committee's predecessor was chaired by the then Leader of the House and back in the mists of time it was chaired by the Prime Minister. That gave the Committee real gravitas, which I believe is now lacking

I do not want to criticise new Members, as those who serve on the Committee are extremely diligent and intelligent, and spend a lot of time examining the evidence, but they lack one huge dimension: experience. Experience counts in such investigations, as it helps one to understand what a Member of Parliament could or could not be expected to know. One needs to have served in the House before one can reach such judgments. The composition of the Committee is all wrong.

We need to ask ourselves whether legal representation should be allowed. In highly complex investigations of the sort that went on in the Hamilton case, we should consider seriously whether we should allow cross-examination of witnesses. It is worth pointing out that in this case Mr. Hamilton was not allowed to cross-examine the witnesses against him, even in front of Sir Gordon Downey, never mind in front of the Committee. That seems to me to be another affront to justice, and even to natural justice.

I do not say that there are easy answers. I am not standing here sanctimoniously saying that we should have had it all sorted out, although we should have had a lot more sorted out than we did;—but the solution that the Committee should have arrived at was to say honestly to the House that within our current remit, against procedures of which we were not even certain, we really needed clearer instructions before we could proceed. As it is, we have left a man who may be guilty—I do not presume innocence—with no clear verdict and no right of appeal. That should bring us deep shame.

It is urgently necessary that the House address itself to what it expects the Committee to do, what composition it should have, and how we are to resolve the situation. It will be fine as long as we carry on having simple cases, but the next time that we get one of the complexity of the Hamilton case, we will be back in exactly the same situation if we have not sorted out our procedures.

I resigned from the Committee because I could not go on wading against a sea of uncertain procedures, with no clear remit, making things up as we went along and, in the end, having to subscribe to a report that, I believe, brought shame on us, not because we had not made honest efforts but because we had not been able to sort out the mess. It ill behoves any Select Committee to return a shambles to the House.

Of course I understand the convention by which both Government and Opposition accept reports from Select Committees, especially when they concern standards and privileges and the regulation of our own conduct; but on this occasion

I believe that they should not have accepted the report: it should have been sent back to the Committee for reconsideration. It was accepted, however, and the damage is done; whether justly or unjustly, we will never know, because there is no appeal. We must get this sorted out for the future. If we cannot regulate ourselves we have absolutely no right to aspire to regulate anybody else.

OCTOBER 1998

Conservative Conference Speech

In 1998 Ann Widdecombe was promoted to the Shadow Cabinet to take on the Health role. In October that year she made her first platform speech at Conservative Party Conference and startled everyone by speaking without notes for forty five minutes while walking up and down the stage like a modern-day evangelist.

* * *

Firstly may I introduce the Conservative Health Team: In the Commons, assisting me is Alan Duncan, our spokesman on public health and dentistry; and Philip Hammond, who has been thinking about social services and pharmaceuticals. In the Lords, we have Lord McColl of Dulwich, who is also an eminent Professor of Surgery at Guy's; and the Earl Howe.

So you can see that although I don't approve of hunting, I do like to keep terriers by me!

Three months ago our Health Service celebrated its 50th Anniversary. This is something that we, as Conservatives, can feel very proud of. After all, two-thirds of the life of our Health Service has been spent in partnership with Conservative governments.

And throughout this period the Conservative record on running and funding our Health Service has been second to none.

That is because the Conservative commitment to the principles of our Health Service is absolute and unbending. And because the Conservatives are, and have always been, 100 per cent committed to the values of our Health Service.

Those values are: Fairness, excellence, decency, innovation.

Our Health Service is not the property of any one party, even though Labour stooped to hijack the 50th anniversary for their own political ends. They tried to use our doctors, our nurses, and our hospitals for their own propaganda.

But don't take my word for our commitment—just look at our record.

In 1979 we inherited from Labour a demoralised and collapsing Health Service. And, to borrow one of Frank Dobson's favourite phrases, we turned round the super-tanker. We gave our Health Service record funding: An average increase of 3.1% in real terms, every year between 1979 to 1997. And I want to take this opportunity to give my personal word that the Conservatives are unshakeably committed to increased funding for our Health Service year on year.

That word is final - we will not waver from it.

We never wavered from our commitment to modernise and revitalise our Health Service. But funding is only a part of it. We also had courage, even when we were being deliberately misconstrued. We put tens of thousands more doctors and nurses on our wards. Slashed patients' waiting times. Financed an ever-growing range of new treatments, and set about Britain's biggest hospital investment programme in history.

We did this because we all depend upon our Health Service. It is a vital part of our nation's sense of security. It is one of the great national institutions that binds us all together.

And it is because we are so passionate about the future of our Health Service that we have the courage to face the facts. To realise and plan for the simple truth that our Health Service has never, and will never be able to meet every last demand for new treatments.

But Labour isn't facing this.

They prefer spin.

Tough choices; difficult debates. They're not happy bedfellows of the good-news, PR driven, cosy culture of this style over substance government. They haven't even got the guts to talk about tough choices, let alone take them or to face the decisions we must take together to make our Health Service the best in the world.

Look at what Labour pledged. Then look at what they have done...

They led Britain to believe that all the problems of our Health Service could be solved by changing the government. That waiting lists would be cut. That hospitals would be saved. That nurses' pay awards wouldn't be staged.

And remember that pledge they made to the patients of our Health Service. That key early pledge to the people of Britain? A pledge made just 18 months ago. Let me remind you what Mr. Blair said: He said that Labour would cut waiting lists by 100,000 with £100 million used from cutting Health Service red tape. That they would 'save' the NHS.

An early pledge to reduce waiting lists, and within 18 months, the pledge broken. Labour pledge—Labour Let Down.

The reality is Labour waiting lists up 100,000 and red tape is choking our Health Service.

As for that £100 million... well they've already wasted four times more than that.

So it's clear now that their early pledge - the "peoples' pledge"—is a portable pledge. A pledge postponed until the next election.

Any businessman who achieved a goal four years late and four times over-budget would find his P45 following by return of post. Well, that is just what this Government will get from the Electorate next time.

Yet Mr. Blair and Mr. Dobson seem to think that we should all be grateful for their performance!

But that's not the worst of it by a long way. Because in their desperation to meet this ill thought out pledge, they have realised that they just can't do it without cheating.

The figures are being fiddled—and patients are hurting as a result.

The BMA realise this. They're telling us that Labour's obsession with the waiting lists is harming clinical priorities. Consultants are being paid large sums of money to perform quick, simple operations ahead of the more complex and often more serious ones. The proof is in the huge increase in the numbers waiting over 12 months. It's political control—not patient care. Some patients are being removed from the waiting lists altogether, without receiving their operations, and others are having to wait longer and longer to get onto the list in the first place.

Well if Frank thinks that he's turned round his super-tanker ... then it looks to me as if it must have Robert Maxwell steering at the helm!

But it won't be Frank who's the man overboard...It will be the motley collection of Labour hacks—Tony's Cronies—that he packed onto our trust boards. They'll be the ones who carry the can for Labour failure, for Frank Dobson has threatened that if he fails to get waiting lists back to the levels of the last Conservative government he'll sack the cronies he appointed.

But after all of that, it's not even as though crude waiting lists are what matters for patients—it's the length of time they spend in the queue, not the number of people in it. That's what matters for patients.

I want to set realistic targets for different disease groups. This may not be so politically convenient, but it will give greater certainty and security to patients. Not Labour's bogus pledge. We've kept our eye on that target - Labour only has eyes for the morning's headlines.

They promised to 'save' our Health Service. And what have we got? We've got record waiting lists, fiddled figures, hospital cuts and closures, GPs coerced into collectives, bureaucracy on the rampage, Tony's Cronies packed onto trust boards. And its all to the background of the slickest spin-doctored public misinformation campaign in the history of our Health Service.

And the result? Just ask the doctors they're dragooning into Primary Care Groups. Ask the nurses how Labour has fiddled their pay review body. Ask the patients waiting in a queue that would stretch more than twice the way round the M25. They'll tell you that morale is at an all-time low. They'll tell you that Labour is more about political control than patient care. They'll tell you Labour's been a let down.

And this goes to the heart of the debate on our Health Service: The expectations Labour whipped up, and their inability to meet them. We all believe that our Health Service should be available to everyone regardless of their ability to pay. We all believe that it should be free at the point of delivery. We all believe that it should be there for everyone when they need it most. I am personally committed to all these principles.

But we can no longer pretend, as Labour continue to do, that it can meet every last demand. To sustain the facade that we can offer every single latest treatment for every single conceivable condition. That we can fund everything patients desire.

There are now two debates on our Health Service. The first is the Facile Debate - the Blairite debate of spin, sound-bite, and pledge. But this is just the empty debate of a PR-mad government engaged in a glib quest for easy solutions, where everything that was wrong with our Health Service was the fault of the Tories, and it only needed the magic wand of New Labour to put it right. Where Frank pretends rationing doesn't exist, and the central problems of rising demand and limited resources are ignored.

Well, we all know what has happened...

The second debate is the Mature Debate. Where we acknowledge the realities of modern medicine. Where we are honest about the fact that our Health Service cannot do it all. Where we recognise what Labour dare not—that piecemeal increases in funding will never keep pace with the exponential growth of technological and clinical change.

But this is too dangerous for New Labour. Whilst they paid lip service to the need for welfare reform, they are still running scared of contemplating reform of our Health Service. They dare not even admit the existence of rationing! I know it's almost too incredible to believe, but Labour's White Paper actually said "we don't find the arguments in favour of rationing to be convincing".

Astonishing, isn't it? But you've got to feel a little bit sorry for Frank. After all, if he doesn't know how many hospitals he is personally closing down, it's not too hard to believe that he's in blissful ignorance of something that's been part of our Health Service for the last 50 years. He doesn't seem to realise that he is making rationing decisions every day. You can't get operations for varicose veins, lipomas, or sebaceous cysts any more in our Health Service on a national basis. And that's to say nothing of Viagra. The reason for mentioning the rationing of Viagra is not that I want you all to have it but that it exemplifies the rationing which poor old Frank denies exists.

So, maybe Frank isn't there to think the unthinkable—well, we all know what happens to the Franks that get that job in this Labour government—but we, at least, are not afraid to start the Mature Debate.

And we are starting that Mature Debate, not by lecturing but by listening.

Listening to doctors; listening to nurses; listening to patients; listening to everyone who cares about the future of our Health Service. We have been learning what we were already beginning to suspect. That we need to look for new and imaginative ways of funding some of the modern healthcare innovations that patients are demanding—the innovations that governments are finding impossible to fund alongside the essential core functions of our Health Service.

But this does not mean charging. The trouble with charges is that they can deter people in genuine need of care. I would never do this. I want public health care to remain free at the point of delivery. Always.

So how are we to produce additional flows of new money into our Health Service?

It means we've got to stop being ideological. This Labour government likes to speak glibly of bringing down 'Berlin Walls' in our Health Service. But at the same time it has been digging a Grand Canyon between the public and private health sectors.

Frank's motives aren't altruistic, but dogmatic. One of his first acts as Health Secretary was to order all our GPs not to use the private sector for their patients. Even if it was cheaper. Even if it was faster. They still just can't bring themselves to accept that private medicine has benefits for the whole community.

Well, unless it suits their own political agenda. At some point after the general election, PFI mysteriously changed from a Tory plot to privatise our Health Service into a massive New Labour investment in hospital building. Yet more spin doctors in the surgery.

Indeed, Frank is even claiming credit for the hospitals we commissioned! Deals signed weeks after the general election.

No. We have to consider the opportunities presented by the private sector - not play the old ideological games of the early 80s. The question is very simple. If we accept that our Health Service cannot do it all, then me must either resign ourselves to ever increasing rationing, which is now happening by stealth, or look to increase the flows of additional new cash into our Health Service though common-sense co-operation with the private sector.

And that isn't just about private insurance, and it's certainly not about patients paying for what they used to get free. It's about the massive investment in pharmaceuticals, research, and clinical technology. It's about PFI helping to fund our hospitals. It's co-operation - not Labour hostility - between our Health Service and private medicine.

Nobody should be bludgeoned into using the private sector. But nobody should be made to feel guilty for using it either. The person who uses private health care frees up the NHS to help someone else. And let's look at the companies and trade unions that have supplied private healthcare for their employees and members - let's look at the costs and the benefits in terms of health care overall. What matters is the the totality of funding, both public and private, devoted to making patients better.

These are issues where we're starting to learn from our listening. These are key components of the Mature Debate. I don't have any prescriptive policies for this conference. The debate is only just beginning.

But to refuse to enter the Mature Debate is to let down our Health Service. It is to stoke up public disillusionment with governments that make so many empty pledges for our Health Service. It is to mislead the public with glib assertions that they can have it all and have it on the cheap. That, of course, is the defining feature of New Labour's approach to our Health Service.

Labour's obsession with the Facile Debate has dominated their policies since coming to power. The ethos of political control is overriding the clinical priorities of patient care, not just in the scandal of the fiddled figures, but in the centralisation of power in our Health Service; in the coercion of our GPs into collectives; in Tony's Cronies packed onto trust boards; in the vacillation over mental health policy.

If you need another example, just look at their politically correct, prescriptive approach to public health. Just remember Formula One. The Nanny State has decreed that tobacco is obviously so dangerous, it can only be advertised on vehicles travelling at over 150 miles per hour!

And it's a pretty vain Nanny at that. The Public Health Minister —Chief Nanny Tessa Jowell, put her photograph no fewer than 32 times in an 18 page booklet on public health.

... Now I could understand it if she had my good looks!

Our nurses are at the heart of our Health Service. And we need to get them back on our wards, not with superficial gimmicks, but by valuing the essential contribution they make to patient care. I'm not just talking about pay - that needs to be resolved alongside all the other issues that have an impact on recruitment and retention. But let me make one thing clear on pay: we will expect the government to implement any recommendation made by the Independent Pay Review Body, as we did consistently.

I have never said the nurses do not deserve a pay rise as the lower end of the tabloid press reports today , but nor will I pluck irresponsible figures out of the air and back any figure, no matter how astronomic. But I will point out that the Review Body is no longer as independent as it was and I shall watch the outcome of its deliberations with interest.

We must acknowledge the changing nature of nursing and the enormous shift in skills over the last decades, along with the increased burden of record-keeping and accountability and technology and training which would have seemed like science fiction thirty years ago.

We need to restore the visible leadership and advocacy for our nurses represented by Matron. She was both a dragon to and a champion of the nurses and we want her back.

We need to make sure that our nurses are encouraged to return to the profession after an extended career break, even though nursing has changed so much.

But Labour won't face these difficult challenges. They make no attempt to address the fundamental issues facing our Health Service. There's just a sinister control-freak mentality, PR gloss and sound-bites.

But this is a bullying government. It's a fiddling, cheating, gerrymandering, dissembling, spin-doctoring, arrogant government for whom getting the headlines have become more important than getting the results.

However, the time of the Facile Debate is running out. It's based on a premise that patients can be fooled continuously. Well they can't.

We're listening to patients. They're telling us—You're telling us—that you want to hear the Mature Debate. That you want to take part. That you want us to hear you.

Well I have a message for you. You have a champion with the Conservative Party. We will listen to, develop, and fight for the mature arguments. Because we believe in our Health Service, and we believe in its future.

Christian Capitalism

In January 1999 Ann Widdecombe preached   at the City of London's New Year Service. Ann, who is opposed to women priests prefers to say she addressed the congregation. The sermon (or address) set out her views on Christian capitalism.

* * *

I am taking as the basis for this address the Parable of the Good Samaritan. It is so well known that it may be pointless to rehearse it but perhaps I could remind you of the essential features of it. A man sets out upon a journey—in those days journeys from town to town could be extremely long ones, perhaps lasting several days or even longer—and in the course of that journey he was attacked, robbed and left severely battered by the wayside. Two pillars of the community passed by on the other side, offering no help. Then a Samaritan came along and bound up his wounds, put him on his own beast—as the authorised version puts it—and took him to an inn, gave the innkeeper some money and said, that if it cost more than that to look after him until he was better, then he, the Samaritan, would pay the innkeeper the amount due when he next passed that way.

The usual interpretation of this Parable is that it was a man from a rather despised area, rather than two pillars of the local Jewish community, who gave the necessary assistance. That, however, is not the aspect on which I wish to dwell. Instead I want to look at this Parable in a rather different light.

In fact, the Parable gives us a model for how society ought to function. It teaches us about the role of compassion, the role of money and the necessity of trust. I am going to focus very heavily on that last point because it is the often ignored lesson of this Parable.

First of all, however, compassion. The Samaritan, we can assume, was himself going about his business but he stopped that business and put first the needs of the man by the wayside, and that teaches us that society should put the needs of those by the wayside first. In modern terms, we need a Health Service and a Social Security system, etc.

Then we are taught about the role of money. The Samaritan had to be able to pay the innkeeper. The lesson for society here is that we have to have money, as well as direct involvement, in order to put compassion into effect. We cannot run a comprehensive health service or a universal education system or an effective pensions system unless we have the money to do so. That is why I believe that capitalism is a very Christian model for society to follow. I am particularly glad to be here in the City today because you make an overwhelming contribution to paying the innkeeper in Britain and, indeed, you pay the world's innkeeper in as much as the wealth which you bring into this country enables us also to assist overseas where people are suffering famine and other deprivation.

The Samaritan in this Parable had a beast. Had he not had a beast he would not have been able to take the man to the inn. Therefore, if anybody tells you to give up your car and go about your business by pedal cycle, you can always retort that you cannot help the man who fell among thieves get to hospital on your pedal cycle! And, indeed, if you have a very large Mayoral car, it will be that much easier to help the man who fell among thieves. Then we see that the Samaritan had wine and oil to help the man as well as a beast on which to assist him to the inn. We should therefore, not be afraid of individual wealth. It is the use to which it is put which matters and which determines whether or not it is morally held.

There are many by the wayside in our society. People who are at this moment lying on trolleys, in fear and pain, awaiting treatment are by the wayside, old age pensioners wondering about stretching their resources to cover extra heating are by the wayside, people sitting desperately in Social Security offices are by the wayside. People in prison, about to be released and wondering how they are going to manage their future lives, are by the wayside. We owe all of them a duty of care and in order to discharge that duty it is not only right but imperative that society creates the necessary wealth in order to afford the systems which underpin compassion.

But let me now turn to the third lesson of this Parable. Trust. Let us see what happened at the end. The Good Samaritan says to the innkeeper, "if I haven't given you enough money, when I next pass I will pay you what I owe you." First of all, the Good Samaritan was trusting the innkeeper. He was trusting the innkeeper not to turf the man out the next day and then to pretend that he had kept him for several days. He was trusting the innkeeper not to over-charge. He was trusting the innkeeper to look after the man in the fashion which they had agreed. The innkeeper was trusting the Good Samaritan, he was trusting him to pass that way again (and it might have been some time before he did so), he was trusting him to pay what he, the innkeeper, demanded and not to haggle. Everybody benefited from this arrangement. The innkeeper benefited from the custom, the Good Samaritan benefited because he was able to go on about his business and not have to wait until the man had recovered and, of course, overwhelmingly, the man who fell among thieves benefited because he was able to get better in a proper fashion, properly provided for.

There is here a tremendous lesson for us in society. We all benefit where there is trust but once trust is broken it is very difficult to repair. I come from a profession which is not particularly trusted by most people! And yet it is essential that people trust those who rule them, that they can have confidence in the intentions and integrity of those whom they elect even if disagreeing with them. It is just as essential that those who rule can trust the ruled. For example, if a State sets up a system of Social Security, it must be able to trust its citizens not to abuse that system. Once the system is widely abused and abuse is taken for granted, it starts to break down and the real sufferers then are the genuinely needy. There has to be trust from the vulnerable towards professionals: people must be able to trust their doctors. If that trust is broken because the doctor abuses the patient or neglects the patient or is otherwise culpable then, again, everybody suffers because faith in a very vital profession breaks down.

And, of course, there must be trust between individuals. The Good Samaritan and the innkeeper did not have agreements signed in triplicate. Their word was sufficient.

Our ancestors had another term for this. They called it "honour" and the concept of honour in society has broken down rather badly. Too few people trust too few other people. We need to regain the concept of trust, of a word being honoured as a matter of principle. It does not matter whether it is called trust or integrity or honour. It is the concept which we need again to be operative, to be the basis on which we do our business.

So, I pray that God will lead you to trust others because, just as in order to be forgiven we have to forgive others, so in order to be trusted we have first to trust others."

1999

The State and Private Morality

In 1998 Ann Widdecombe wrote the introduction to the Inner Temple Year Book which was subsequently reprinted in the Salisbury Review.

* * *

Private and Public morality are not always easily distinguishable as the morals of the individual have a significant impact on society as a whole. What two fully consenting adults do in private is their business unless and until the consequence affects others on a scale which makes it appropriate for the State to take a view. In this context it is impossible for individuals to regard their actions as purely private if they are contributing to a sum of activity or attitudes which militates against stability and order in society as a whole.

It is common ground among most serious commentators that the breakdown of the traditional family has had profoundly undesirable social consequences contributing to increased youth crime, greater dependency on welfare benefits, confused and insecure childhoods and a strain on social housing. Inadequate parenting becomes the too frequent consequence of children growing up with no stable male role model.

If this is the case then the State has a legitimate interest in promoting a preferred model for the upbringing of children and therefore it follows that it also has a legitimate interest in discouraging lifestyles which do not conform to this model.

How far should the State go in protecting society as a whole from the consequences of the moral choices of a large minority? Or even a majority? If it is right to discourage is it right also to outlaw? Indeed is there a moral imperative to criminalise some moral choices?

I believe that in some cases there is such an imperative but before examining those questions we need first to look at the duty of the State to protect the vulnerable and, in particular, the young. There has long been a consensus that young people should not be allowed to take certain actions until they can fully appreciate the consequences. Hence the criminal law forbids the purchase of cigarettes or alcohol before a certain age and specifies a minimum age of consent to sexual activity or marriage and for the driving of motor vehicles. Access to certain types of film or video material is similarly restricted.

In some of these examples it is possible to draw a clear distinction between the private and the public act. The purchase of alcohol for a minor is an offence in a public restaurant but it is not unlawful to allow the same minor to consume alcohol at home. In other cases there is patent confusion within the law. Thus sexual activity below the age of consent is unlawful, but the prescription of contraceptives for an under age girl by a General Practitioner is not.

There are plenty of current issues which pose questions about the rightness of State interference in individual moral choices: the homosexual age of consent, foxhunting, drug-taking, euthanasia and film censorship to name but a few.

I return to my original proposition: that if the effects of such choices are sufficiently widely adverse then the State must discourage them and if it is right to discourage then there must be occasions when it is also right to outlaw.

However the law can be a blunt instrument and presupposes enforcement. That can make it not only an undesirable but an impractical weapon for the State to use. Once a principle is enshrined in law there is a presumed intolerance of its violation. Using the law to enforce the State's preferred model of adult sexual behaviour has a bad history of misery, blackmail, absurdity and plain unenforceability.

To tolerate while promoting the alternative is a better option. It sends a clear signal while not making a pariah of the non-conforming. Fiscal incentives send signals but it is dubious if they alter moral behaviour a very great deal. A strong example of good moral conduct in public life sends signals but is hardly a defining influence. It is consensus which makes the difference—when there is a widely shared view of what is or is not acceptable. Forty years ago such consensus was not hard to seek. Today the only thing which is not tolerated is intolerance.

Let us look at one issue which will be before Parliament in this session - homosexual age of consent. The arguments for and against lowering it to bring it into line with the heterosexual age of consent draw together all the threads in the foregoing paragraphs: the protection of the young, the preferred model, the use of law, the sending by the State of signals, the existence of a consensus.

Let us start with the preferred model. No satisfactory substitute has ever been found for the traditional family in which children are raised against the background, of a stable relationship - between two adults of opposite sexes - publicly recognised by marriage. The widespread breakdown of that pattern has produced the results to which I alluded at the beginning of this article. Therefore the State finds it to be in the interests of society generally to promote that model.

Homosexuality falls without that model and will not therefore be promoted, but does that mean it must be restricted? Thirty years ago it was unlawful for two fully consenting adults to perform homosexual acts in private. The result was a great deal of misery and not much benefit to anyone. So the State withdrew from interfering in private morality and decriminalised such practices. There was still a consensus which upheld the traditional family as the standard to aim for and the law protected the young by setting an age of consent of twenty one.

What was missing was tolerance. Something can be legal and still be feared and ridiculed. Thus it was with homosexuality. A kinder view was yet to develop.

Greater understanding does not, however, mean according whatever is tolerated equal validity with what is preferred and that lies at the heart of the debate about the homosexual age of consent. The overwhelming majority of parents still want their children to grow up with the prospect of marriage and having children of their own. The State therefore is in tune with the general consensus but how far should it intervene? What is the merit of continuing an unequal age of consent?

The merit is in the signal it sends, in the protection of the young, in promoting the preferred model of the traditional family. So long as there is evidence that a sixteen year old is not generally ready to take decisions about actions which might set him apart from most of his peers and which might expose him to the exploitation of ill intentioned adults the State has a duty to maintain a higher age of consent.

What about those areas of State intervention which prohibit young and old alike? The most obvious example is the illegality of drugs, whether hard or soft. Is the State trying to protect the citizen from himself or to protect society as a whole? The answer must be both. Drug taking leads to crime, both that committed while under the influence of drugs and that which is committed to finance a drug habit, it also leads to ill health, unemployability and a drain on the tax payer. The debate about decriminalisation is not only about libertarianism but also about practicality. Arguments are deployed to the effect that usage and therefore abuse would be easier to control if it could be done in the open.

Practicality aside, the libertarian argument is simply that soft drugs are harmless and it is therefore inappropriate for the State to intervene in a harmless private activity. Yet so strict is the law that the police will invade private property and prosecute anyone possessing drugs therein if necessary. By contrast people may drink themselves incapable and commit no offence if it is done in private.

In this case the law is not only sending signals and protecting the young, rather it is a weapon of intolerance which springs from the need to defend society as a whole from the corrupting effects of widespread drug use.

Yet it does not do the same with alcohol and cigarettes despite their own contribution to crime and ill health. Smoking is gradually becoming the victim of a growing consensus of intolerance but alcohol is unscathed by social disapproval, much to the relief of the author who likes her whisky and soda. What justifies the distinction? Practicality does. An unenforceable law is an ineffective law and the State has no chance of a successful intervention in smoking or drinking, though it has a duty to inform and to educate. If, however, neither of these substances had a long history of legality it is unlikely they would be tolerated in today's health conscious climate. Their widespread use is, however, an argument for not against criminalising cannabis or other drugs of that nature. After all, why enlarge a problem?

Now let us look at a tougher question. Is it right that the State should oblige anyone to suffer without hope of survival or relief from pain when there is an alternative route which that individual wishes to take? Should the State so far intrude into private morality that its laws obviate a peaceful death? If someone is terminally and painfully ill and wishes to cut short the suffering and a doctor is of his own free will agreeable to help and if the death of that person is of no detriment to society as a whole and all the relatives are on side what on earth right does the law have to intervene and enforce a lingering death?

I believe, with some reluctance, that it does have that right and that belief is not founded in my private religious views so much as in my observation of what happens when the law takes a back seat on these matters.

In 1967 the abortion laws in this country were liberalised and we were all assured that this would not lead to abortion on demand or a decline in respect for unborn life or pressure on medical staff to become involved in abortion against their conscience. Five million abortions later those claims look hollow. It was the same with the divorce laws in 1969. We were told liberalisation would not lead to the breakdown of the institution of marriage or to widespread divorce and now forty per cent of marriages end in divorce. In 1968 we were told the decriminalisation of homosexuality would not lead to its active promotion a prophecy which is scarcely fulfilled by the necessity of clause 28 in the Local Government Act.

The issue here is not whether one thinks it a good or bad thing that these have been the effects of those laws; rather the issue is that quite undeniably the effects were not foreseen. For that reason I believe that if we were to legalise voluntary euthanasia then, no matter how tightly the law was framed, in ten years time no Granny would be safe. If I am right then the State has an appropriate role in this sphere also.

Perhaps the real issue is: is there any such thing as private morality other than what goes on in one's head or does moral conduct always have a public dimension? Can any man be a moral island?

The answer must be that sometimes he can but often he is not and when his actions add to a sum of instability the State can send signals that it would prefer otherwise while still tolerating those actions. It can still tolerate but at the same time reward and penalise. In some cases it can and should cast aside tolerance and criminalise. All those measures can be justified if the ill consequences of not taking them are great enough but in the end it is consensus which is the most potent force in protecting both individual and State.

An After Dinner Speech

Ann Widdecombe is a sought after speaker on the Conservative after dinner circuit. As she always speaks without notes there is no actual speech but here she recreates one for us.

* * *

Well, thank you very much for that kind introduction. It is better than the one I received at a function like this the other day' when the Chairman said, "And now we come to Ann Widdecombe who recently impressed the entire Conservative conference with her debatable qualities." Even that is an improvement on the one I often get when whoever is introducing me refers to my Christian principles. That always causes me to wince.

During the last Election I produced a leaflet called "Standing Up For Christian Principles". On one occasion I was in the very busy centre of Maidstone - the whole town was packed with constituents and other people who were not going to vote for me - on a Saturday morning and my agent having just transferred a whole lot of literature from his car to mine was driving away when I noticed I did not have any of that particular leaflet. Thereupon half Maidstone heard me hail on my loudspeaker "Brian! Come back! I haven't got any Christian principles!"

I am always a bit dubious about speaking after so good a meal. That is because not very long ago I was asked to address a similarly convivial function and about two seconds into my speech I noticed a gentleman at a nearby table nod off. It would not have mattered so much had the title of my speech not been "Wake up to the dangers of Blair". Every so often I would enumerate these dangers, cry "We must wake up to this" and pause dramatically. Into the pause would come a gentle snore from where this character sat.

When I sat down, not even the customary applause managed to wake him up but I would not have given it a further thought until the Chairlady looked straight at him and said "I now call upon Mr.X to give the vote of thanks."

That chap should have been a politician. He was woken up very violently by the people either side of him and shot to his feet still waking up. He immediately realised that he had been sound asleep, that everyone knew he had been asleep, that he had nothing to thank me for because he had not heard a word I had said and that there was huge curiosity as to how he was going to get out of the situation. He only paused a second before saying, with great aplomb, "Miss Widdecombe, thank you very much for that dream of a speech."

Now, we are going to win next time aren't we? (Audience say "Yes"). Let's try again. We are going to win aren't we? (audience shout "yes"). Once more. (audience bellow " Yes").

That's right and that is how we have got to sound, because if we do not look as if we mean it and sound as if we mean it and above all act as if we mean it then no one else is going to believe it. From now on we do not want people to say "Oh, what a good opposition". We want people to say "Oh, what a good government in waiting".

First don't let anybody tell you winning is impossible. Don't get into the habit of thinking "well, it would be nice to win next time but really we will win the time after." Sometimes even good, loyal, hardworking Conservatives think like that and worse still talk like that. Forget it. If we lose next time and Tony Blair thinks he is going to lose the time after he will get together with the Liberals and alter the Electoral system in this country to make sure Britain can never have an outright Conservative Government again. We are in a grim primeval struggle for the survival of the species and the species in question are Conservative Government and the future democracy of our electoral system.

And of course we can win. Blair did not, contrary to popular perception, get a great landslide swing to Labour. I know it feels as if he did but the solid, undeniable fact is that Labour got fewer votes last time than we did in 1992. Our vote stayed at home and if it was not prepared to switch to Labour last time I see no reason why it should do so now, let alone after another two years of this lot in power. So there is everything to play for in getting it back.

I know he has a great mountain of a majority in Parliament: I sit and look at it every day and apart from David Blunkett's guide dog, a pretty ghastly sight it is. But that majority is made up of individual majorities some of which are just a few hundred and many more just a few thousand. Those majorities will go in the first puff of adverse wind for this government and I am not interested in puffs - I want us to create one heck of a hurricane.

So we can win. But we have to change "can" to "will".

That means two things: vigorous, unremitting opposition and honest, imaginative proposition.

I know the last couple of years have been dispiriting but they were always going to be. It was always going to be the case that, after eighteen long years in power and having been dismissed on the scale we were dismissed on in 97, we were going to have to expect to be marginalised for a while. All the interest, all the good will, all the benefit of the doubt was going to go to the new, untried, incoming Government not to the one that had been there eighteen years. It was utterly inevitable that the focus of press and media would be the new not the old. It was hopelessly unrealistic to expect that somehow we were going to look like a Government in waiting by the middle of Tuesday afternoon.

No amount of charisma, no amount of activity, no amount of bright ideas could have saved us from those first couple of years but it was also equally inevitable that, providing we kept our nerve and our principles, the situation would not go on forever. Disillusionment would gradually replace euphoria, then disillusionment would deepen into anger and then people would ask where and what is the alternative. Disillusionment is beginning. Look at the local elections, at the Euro elections, at Eddisbury. Blair promised a very great deal and is not delivering. He said Labour was whiter than white and they have been immersed in sleaze and scandal: Lord Simon, Robin Cook, Ron Davies, Geoffrey Robinson, Peter Mandelson. They have produced more impropriety in two years than we managed in twenty.

Our job is now to deepen that disillusionment. We must expose tirelessly every failure to honour pledges, for example, in the Health Service where the numbers waiting to see the Consultants have risen drastically, where the numbers waiting more than twelve months for an operation have risen, where choice has been reduced and the Service swamped by reorganisation and bureaucracy. We must not let them get away with any trick or treachery such as fiddling figures. We must be eternally vigilant and examine the implications, line by line, of all their legislation. And we must make sure Britain knows.

That is opposition. But we also need proposition - that is to say policy, so that when people look to see if we offer an alternative we can convince them that we do. I acknowledge that the last two and a half years have been tough for you in that respect also. You have had to go on doorsteps without slick, easy, brightly packaged pledges. I am afraid, however, that we were right to do that to you.

I know you have all had a splendid meal and a relaxed evening and that this is not the moment to ask you to do anything unpleasant but nevertheless may I ask you, just for a minute, to

128

think about Neil Kinnock. Do you remember that the way he ran his opposition was to make a policy pronouncement a minute right from the start and the result was that years later, when the General Election came along, he was locked into a hideously expensive and hopelessly inappropriate agenda. We might avoid the extravagance but if we had pronounced too soon we could not have avoided irrelevance because the trick in opposition is not to make policy for the world as it was when you lost but for the world as it will be when you next fight and therefore a wise Opposition keeps its powder dry for the first half of a Parliament.

However that period too is over and policy pronouncements will soon start.

What sort of pronouncements? I believe they must be honest, imaginative and Conservative.

First, honest. Labour spent eighteen years telling lies, pretending they had magic wands to wave over health, education and crime; that all that was necessary was to change the Government and a bit of goodwill and extra cash would solve it all. We must not make that mistake. We must tell the truth: that, for example, no matter how much extra we spend on health we will never spend enough and that unless we have real partnership with the private sector and start using its money and resources as well there will simply be too much demand and too little supply; that it is not possible to put a policeman on every street corner; that criminals will not suddenly change their ways just because they have been sent to prison and that it is what you do with them while they are which makes the difference; that the State can not do it all; that the public has a duty towards government as well as government towards people; that there are no magic wands.

I know the public do not want to hear this but nor do they need the spin and smoke and mirrors stuff Labour is giving them daily. They are not deceived and they are certainly not fools. They will respect truth. We must give it to them.

Second, imaginative. I have a vision for our health service

education service, our prisons, our provision for old age, for the role everybody must play in creating a better, thriving, orderly, kinder Britain. None of it can be brought about by promises, a bit of extra spending and a bit of tinkering, by pledging to be nice to everyone and expecting nothing from anybody beyond a vote. Our next manifesto must be a breath of fresh air.

Third, Conservative. You may say that is obvious but it still needs saying. We do not need to do what Tony Blair has done and simply give up every principle and political belief we ever had. After all if we got it so very wrong why did Tony Blair have to adopt so much of our agenda in order to get elected? The fact is Britain wanted our agenda at the same time as deciding it had had enough of us. So we need to offer the same underlying principles: loyalty to the Union not to fragmenting the UK; defence of individual freedom and the right to choose, for example, grammar schools, doctors, consultants; encouragement for small businesses; less bureaucracy for all businesses; standing up for ourselves in Europe; a resolute approach to crime.We need to update our policies, modernise the packaging, learn the lessons of the past but still stick to our principles because they are also the principles of those who vote for us.

And then we will win, win, win. If we mean it. If we really mean it. We can and we must not just for our sake but for Britain's. And it will be your victory for it will be based upon your hard work. Thank you for never deserting us, for sticking by us when times were bad. Your reward is imminent. Until now I have said, keep a steady nerve, keep your powder dry, watch the enemy until the moment comes.

Now the moment has come and I now say attack! Forward! Take no prisoners! Cast down that over-mighty, conceited, lying, sleazy failure of a Government from its seat. And give it a good boot as it goes.

Also Available From Politico's Publishing

Dictionary of Conservative Biography
Edited by Mark Garnett
£25.00 Hardback, March 2000

Political insider Mark Garnett brings together, in one volume, the bigraphies of more than 300 individuals who have made major contributions to the Conservative Party or to conservative thought in the 19th and 20th centuries.

Significant essays have been contributed by senior academics and Conservative politicians covering many of Britain's most important historical figures including Margaret Thatcher, Winston Churchill, Disreali, Salisbury, Peel and Chamberlain.

This book is part of a three part series together with the **Dictionary of Liberal Biography** and the **Dictionary of Labour Biography.**

Dictionary of Conservative Quotations
Edited by Iain Dale
£18.00 Hardback, September 1999

The Dictionary of Conservative quotations contains more than 2000 key quotations from important figures in the history of the Conservative Party and conservative political thought.

Ranging from Disraeli to William Hague, from Edmund Burke to Roger Scruton this compendium will be a vital reference source to anyone interested in the Conservative Party or the influence of conservatism on British politics.

This book is part of a three part series together with the **Dictionary of Liberal Quotations** and the **Dictionary of Labour Quotations.**

Great Speeches in Parliament
£21.99 Video
£12.99 Cassette
£16.99 CD
September 1999

Produced in cooperation with the Parliamentary Broadcasting Unit this production is a celebration of ten years of the televisation of Parliament.

Featuring more than three hours of material, the subject matter ranges from fox hunting to gay rights, from welfare to defence. Featuring John Major, Margaret Thatcher, John Smith, Paddy Ashdown, Geoffrey Howe, Norman Lamont and dozens of less well known MPs, this production threatens to become the cult political hit of the year.

The other videos from Politicos Publishing are: **Party Political Broadcasts the Greatest Hits, American Political Commercials the Greatest Hits, New Labour in Focus** with Tony Benn and **Tony Benn Speaks**

Classic Politics
£12.99 Cassette
£16.99 CD
September 1999

In this recording todays politicians read the classic works that inspired tham to enter the world of politics. Featuring many well known politicians including Ann Widdecombe, William Hague, John Redwood, Paddy Ashdown, Edward Heath and many more, the recording covers the full range of political thought from Thomas Paine to Ronald Reagan.

This recording is sure to become one of the cult hits of 1999 and is the ideal stocking filler for political junkies.

To buy these books and many others, new and second hand or to get a copy of our free catalogue visit:

Politico's Bookstore and Coffee House
8 Artillery Row
Westminster
London
SW1P 1RZ

Visit our web-site: www.politicos.co.uk
Phone us on: 020 7828 0010
Fax us on: 020 7828 8111
E-mail us at politicos@artillery-row.demon.co.uk

With thousand of political books, think tank reports, magazines, cards, cds, cassettes, videos, and pictures to choose from, a huge stock of political memorabilia and the best coffee and cakes in London, political junkies have never had it so good.